Delivered From Evil

Jesus' Victory Over Satan

Delivered From Evil
Jesus' Victory Over Satan

The teaching of St. Leo the Great
in a modern version by

Anne Field, O.S.B.

PUBLISHED BY ST. ANTHONY MESSENGER PRESS
CINCINNATI, OHIO

Scripture citation on page 12 marked (NIV) is taken from the *Holy Bible, New International Version* ®. Copyright ©1973, 1978, 1984 by International Bible Society. Used by permission of Zondervan. All rights reserved. All other Scripture citations have been taken from the *New Revised Standard Version Bible: Catholic Edition*, copyright 1993 and 1989 by the Division of Christian Education of the National Council of the Churches of Christ in the United States of America. Used by permission. All rights reserved.

Library of Congress Cataloging-in-Publication Data

Field, Anne M., O.S.B.
  [Binding of the strong man]
  Delivered from evil : Jesus' victory over Satan / Anne Field.
      p. cm.
  ISBN 0-86716-636-3 (alk. paper)
  1. Leo I, the Great, Saint, Pope, 461. 2. Spiritual warfare. 3. Jesus Christ—Person and offices. I. Title.

BR65.L46F54 2005
234'.3—dc22

                    2004030402

Cover design by Cynthia Dunne
Book design by Emily Schneider
Cover painting: Duccio, *Temptation of Christ on the Mountain*
Copyright The Frick Collection, New York
Used by permission.

ISBN 0-86716-636-3

Published by Servant Books.
Servant Books is an imprint of St. Anthony Messenger Press.
28 W. Liberty St.
Cincinnati, Ohio 45202
www.AmericanCatholic.org

Printed in the United States of America.
Printed on acid-free paper.

05 06 07 08 09 8 7 6 5 4 3 2 1

When a strong man, fully armed,
guards his castle, his property is safe.
But when one stronger than he
attacks him and overpowers him,
he takes away his armor in which
he trusted and divides his plunder.

LUKE 11:21-22

CONTENTS

INTRODUCTION

Although in every age many of the troubles that afflict humankind are undoubtedly due to human greed, selfishness, pride and ambition, there has always been a consciousness of more than human forces opposing the coming of the kingdom of God on earth. Not only are people outwardly disturbed by ideological clashes, destructive forces, corruption, graft, violence, child abuse and terrorist threats on a global scale, but they are also inwardly subject to fears and compulsions of every kind. How many are held in unwilling bondage to drugs, alcohol, sex or psychological disorders; how many are captive to a fascination for pornography or the occult; how many are confused and led astray by seductive new teachings; and how many are crippled by feelings of guilt and worthlessness! These are the things that rob the children of God of their freedom. In spite of the contemporary rejection of the notion of a personal devil as a remnant of medieval mumbo-jumbo, there is plenty of evidence pointing to the reality of the evil one and to the conflict between Christianity and the powers of darkness.

In such a climate the Scriptures remind us that our struggle is not against flesh and blood but against the sovereignties and powers that are the source of darkness in this world, against malign influences in the supernatural order (Eph 6:12). Jesus did not hesitate to refer to Satan as a murderer from the beginning, calling him the father of lies (Jn 8:44), the treacherous and cunning enemy of our salvation. But it was to undo the devil's handiwork that the Son of God appeared (Jn 3:8). Jesus has destroyed the power of the evil one and delivered us from his clutches, giving to all who believe in him a share in his victory and making them members of his own body.

"I am the light of the world," Jesus told his disciples. "Whoever follows me will never walk in darkness" (Jn 8:12). For two thousand years those who have followed him have borne witness to the unquenchable faith of the Christian community in the victory Jesus Christ has won over sin and death, and in the reality of the new life he offers to all who are willing to receive it. It is a faith that the powers of darkness have constantly attacked by means of open hostility, subtle persuasion, ridicule or indifference, yet there has never been a time since Pentecost when the Good News of our salvation was not preached. But the problems of a divided Christendom and growing secularism have frequently kept the churches on the defensive, struggling to maintain their hold on a population that finds their message simply irrelevant.

There have been times in the past when an over-systematic, cerebral approach to theology and a spirituality giving greater emphasis to patient resignation than to expectant faith have obscured the joy of the Good News. But when we go back to the era of the Fathers of the Church and encounter this joyful vitality in their writing, we realize what a treasure we already have in our ancient heritage, a treasure buried perhaps under a mound of linguistic difficulties, modes of thought and figures of speech belonging to a different mentality from ours. It takes patience to extract the rich teaching of those early centuries from long-dead controversies, diatribes against heretics, and a style of scriptural exegesis toward which our contemporaries are often unsympathetic.

For this reason, the teaching of the Fathers is not always readily available to the ordinary reader. But "the master of a household . . . brings out of his treasure what is new and what is old" (Mt 13:52), and while the Spirit of Pentecost is continually leading believers into the fullness of truth, giving to later generations insights unsuspected by the early Fathers, we can still be inspired by the vigor of the latter's faith, by their broad, deep understanding of the great mysteries of our redemption, by their overall view of salvation history, and by their practical advice on spiritual warfare.

During the 1970s I was engaged in the translation of a collection of patristic texts for a monastic lectionary. One day I was sitting at my desk when my eyes were suddenly held fast by a sentence from one of the sermons of St. Leo the Great which I had just written down: "The sole aim of all Christ did and suffered was our salvation, and the communication to his members of the power that belongs to him as head" (*Sermon XV on the Passion*). The words seemed to be written with large letters, imbued with that very power of which they spoke. Here was that parting promise of the Lord Jesus to his disciples: "But you will receive power when the Holy Spirit has come upon you" (Acts 1:8). I looked at Leo's teaching with new eyes. The nobility of his thought, the balanced symmetry of his style and the sonorous beauty of his Latin cadences had always appealed to me. Now I realized how powerful was his presentation of the Good News of the gospel. In passage after passage Leo speaks of how, as members of Christ's body, we share in his victory over Satan, his conquest of death, his risen life, his triumphant return to the Father, the gift of his Spirit. The powers of darkness have been overthrown by the cross of Christ, and those who put their faith in the Lord have nothing to fear from the evil one. The events of Christ's life are not simply a matter of past history; they are operative here and now in those who believe. "If we do not hesitate to believe what our lips profess," Leo says, "then not only has Christ died and been raised to life for us, but in Christ we too have been crucified, in him we have died and have been buried, and on the third day we have been raised to life again" (*Sermon II on the Resurrection*).

Leo's teaching has come down to us from fifth century Rome. He was elected pope in A.D. 440, a time when the traditional faith of the Christian Church was under fire from more than one quarter, as it is in our own day. Throughout his pontificate he was absorbed in strenuously opposing one heresy after another, guarding the people of God from errors which would rob them of the freedom Jesus Christ had won for them at the cost of his own blood. These heresies were subtle and confusing to simple souls, and as bishop and pastor Leo used all his knowledge and insight to instruct them in the true faith about the incarnation of the Son of God and the work of our redemption. He never tired of explaining to them that

> the great mystery of the incarnation is that true man is in the God whom no suffering can touch, and true God in the human flesh that is subject to pain and sorrow. By this wonderful exchange man gains glory through shame, immortality through chastisement, life through death. For unless the Word of God were so firmly joined to our flesh that the two natures could not be parted even in death, we mortals would never be able

> to return to life. But when the Lord became one of us
> and died for our sake, death lost its everlasting hold
> over us; through the nature that was undying in Jesus
> Christ, the nature that was mortal was raised to life.
> (*Sermon XIX on the Passion*)

Leo's formula of two natures and one person in Christ provided the basis upon which the Council of Chalcedon subsequently drew up its precise presentation of Jesus Christ, God and Man. Although these terms may seem rather abstract to Christians in these days, they safeguard the faith of the Church in the Jesus of the Gospels, in whom God really and truly entered into human history and accomplished our salvation. Only upon this foundation has the Church's understanding of her Lord and Savior been free to develop.

The substance of Leo's teaching is contained in a collection of sermons preached on the important days of the liturgical year and in a number of letters. Some favorite topics of contemporary interest are touched only lightly if at all—for example, the development of Jesus' human consciousness, or the role of the Holy Spirit in enlightening him about the nature of his mission. There are also a number of patristic themes with which he would have been familiar, but which are not included in his extant writings. The charismatic gifts are mentioned without elaboration. But the confrontation between Jesus and Satan, the conquest of sin and death, the spiritual armor of Christians, the power in praise and in the Word of God, the lordship of Jesus and our life in the Spirit—upon all these subjects Leo has a great deal to say to us today.

It seemed to me that it would be worth the effort to try

to make his teaching more easily accessible. I have tried in the following pages to synthesize it and present it in simple language, eliminating any reference to errors which are no longer fashionable, freely editing and rearranging the material so as to make a more or less straightforward sequence out of the contents of the sixty-odd homilies preached between Christmas and Pentecost. Rather than overburden the text, I have reluctantly omitted many beautiful passages which are only variations on themes already stated. While I have not hesitated to express Leo's ideas in the contemporary idiom or to amplify them here and there, I do not think I have added anything that is outside the range of his thought. If there are places where the line of thought does not seem to follow consecutively, the fault must be laid at my door, not at that of one of the most clear-sighted and logical of the Latin Fathers.

I acknowledge gratefully the support of my abbess and community in this undertaking, together with the encouragement and help of many good friends, especially Bert Ghezzi, Nick Cavnar and Cindy Cavnar of Servant Books. For help with this new edition my thanks also go to Lisa Biedenbach and her colleagues at St. Anthony Messenger Press. It has been good to work with them all.

Stanbrook Abbey
May 2004

CHAPTER ONE

The Strong Man Challenged
Advent and Christmas

✣

WE HAVE PASSED FROM DEATH TO LIFE

> Therefore we have been buried with him by baptism
> into death, so that, just as Christ was raised from the
> dead by glory of the Father, so we too might walk in
> newness of life.... We know that our old self was cruci-
> fied with him so that the body of sin might be
> destroyed, and we might no longer be enslaved to sin.
> (Rom 6:4, 6)

In this tremendous sixth chapter of his Letter to the Romans,
St. Paul asserts that our dying and rising with Christ is an
accomplished fact. It is not something we have to achieve by
our own efforts; it comes to us as pure gift, a gift to be
accepted by faith in all that the Lord has done for us. When
we were baptized and put our faith in the Lord Jesus, we left
our old self-centered existence behind and entered upon a
new life. Our task now is not to earn this new life but to live

it, to enter into the riches of Christ's redemptive work and to allow the paschal mastery of his death and resurrection to enter into our daily lives; for when the Lord Jesus took his seat at the right hand of the Father, he poured out his Spirit on his Church, the Spirit whose mission it is to make available to all believers the salvation Christ has won for us.

The power of the redemption is available to us here and now

Each year the Church unfolds the whole mystery of Christ from his incarnation and birth to his ascension and the day of Pentecost. In this way his redemptive work is made present to us here and now; by our faith we can lay hold of its power and be filled with Christ's own life. The things that Jesus did and taught for the world's reconciliation are not simply a matter of past history. They are fully operative now in those who believe in him. The events of his earthly life contain a divine power, and that power has been communicated to the Church which is his body, so that when the whole body together commemorates those events in the yearly cycle of the liturgy, they are made present in a special way, and the power which is, as it were, encapsulated in them is released and communicated to all his members.

It is true that Jesus, the Son of God, was born at a particular moment in history. He grew up in Nazareth, matured to manhood, then suffered and died; with his resurrection from the dead the labors he had undertaken for us in the humble conditions of a human being were completed. Yet because all the mysteries of his life are made timelessly present to us in the liturgy, the entire body of believers is crucified with Christ on Good Friday, raised up with him at Easter and set at the Father's right hand with him at the ascension. Although we are called one by one to become members of the Lord's body and may be separated from each other by time and space, once we are born anew in baptism we share Christ's life all together, and the whole body together shares in his Passover. Renouncing the devil, professing faith in God, passing from the old life to the new, casting off the image of the earthly man and putting on the heavenly—all this is a dying and rising again. Christians are not the same after baptism as they were before: the bodies of the baptized have become the body of the crucified Christ. It is Christ who lives and acts in them. As they have died with him and have been buried and raised to life with him, so they bear him within them, both in body and spirit, in everything they do.

GOD MADE US REFLECT HIS LIKENESS

If we think for a while about God's plan for the creation of the human race and the way he has made us in his own image, we begin to understand that we are meant to be like a mirror reflecting his likeness in all its beauty and goodness. We know only too well, however, that this reflection is obscured and tarnished by all kinds of obstacles within ourselves. The nature we inherited from Adam is a wounded and fallen one, and unless it is healed and raised up again by Christ, the second Adam, there is nothing we can do of ourselves to become what we are meant to be.

But in his great mercy, God himself has saved and restored us. Because he first loved us and sent the light of his truth to penetrate the darkness of our ignorance and misery, we are now able to love and praise him. Long ago he foretold our salvation in the words of the prophet Isaiah: "I will lead the blind by a way they do not know, by paths they have not known, I will guide them. I will turn the darkness before them into light and the rough places into level ground. These are the things I will do, and I will not forsake them" (Is 42:16). "I was ready to be sought out by those who did not ask," God says, "to be found by those who did not seek me" (Is 65:1). St. John tells us how these prophecies have been fulfilled. "And we know that the Son of God has come," he says, "and has given us understanding so that we may know him who is true; and we are in him who is true, in his Son Jesus Christ.... We love because he first loved us" (1 Jn 5:20; 4:19).

We were all helpless captives

How right it is for us to rejoice in the Lord and to praise our God for the wonderful things he has done, when we realize what store our Maker set by his poor creatures! He not only made us in his own image; he took even greater trouble to restore that likeness when we had spoiled it. Everything he does for us proves his fatherly love, but the sight of God coming down to earth is a far greater wonder than that of humans making their way up to heaven. For unless the Lord had come down to us, no brand of holiness or wisdom could have rescued anyone on earth from bondage to Satan or raised anyone up from everlasting death. The guilt handed on to us by the first human beings would still remain with us, and our wounded nature, powerless to change its own condition, would be unable to find any remedy. After humankind had lost the freedom and innocence of their natural state through the sin of their first parents, no one on earth, no matter how personally blameless, could regain it by his or her own efforts. The curse pronounced against Adam and Eve was binding on the whole of their posterity; the entire human race was condemned to death. "Therefore, just as sin entered the world through one man, and death through sin, and in this way death came to all men, because all sinned" (Rom 5:12 NIV).

When Adam's body was fashioned from the earth, a living soul was breathed into it by his Creator. If the first man had obeyed God and preserved the dignity with which he had been endowed, this spiritual part of his makeup would have lifted up the material part with itself to heavenly glory. But he listened to the deceiver and was taken in by his suggestions. He thought he could forestall the hour and win the honor that was in store for him without first having to undergo probation. Because he did this, he condemned not only himself but every man and woman who came after him. The same verdict was pronounced upon all of humankind: "You are dust, and to dust you shall return" (Gn 3:19). St. Paul tells us that all of us on earth are as that earthly man was; no one is immortal, because no one is heavenly by nature (cf. 1 Cor 15:48-49).

Before Christ came we were all in hopeless bondage to sin, tied hand and foot, blinded by ignorance and folly. We were consumed with a hunger for truth, but the father of lies deceived us by an array of shifting opinions, and we were dragged into all sorts of conflicting notions; our minds were taken captive to serve the devil's pride. The Law of Moses was insufficient for our deliverance; the exhortations of the prophets could not heal us; moral precepts were

powerless to get to the root of our sins. Something more rad-
ical was necessary: we had to be redeemed and born anew.
Instead of the repeated sacrifices of lambs, calves and goats
prescribed by the law, a victim had to be offered for us who
would be one of ourselves but free from our contamination.

God planned our salvation from the beginning

Although humankind had to wait many centuries for their
Savior, God's merciful plan did not exclude the generations
that lived and died before Jesus was born. He had never for-
gotten his people, even in the centuries before he sent his
Son to save them. It was not as if, after long ages, he suddenly remembered us and took pity on us. He had planned
our salvation from the beginning of the world. The redemption which Christ brought was to work backward as well as
forward, through the common faith of all believers. We who
live today believe that his blood has been shed for the
world's reconciliation; the people of the old covenant
believed that it would be shed. Living by this faith, they
received the gift of everlasting life just as we do today.

The light of Christ, it is true, was only a pale glimmer in
Old Testament times, hidden behind symbols and figures
foreshadowing the reality to come. Yet there was never any
other hope of salvation for the world apart from him. The
Christian faith is the fulfillment of the Jewish religion. The
Mosaic Law, with its prescriptions and rituals and the ancient
prophecies and the animal sacrifices of the Old Testament, all
throw light on this same truth. They were given to the children of Israel to prepare them for the gospel, and to make it
easier for them to recognize their Savior in the signs and mysteries contained in the Scriptures.

The Old Testament is full of words and signs foreshadowing our Redeemer. For instance, there was the prophecy made to Abraham: "And by your offspring shall all the nations of the earth gain blessings for themselves" (Gn 22:18). There was the promise made to David: "The LORD swore to David a sure oath from which he will not turn back: / 'One of the sons of your body I will set on your throne,'" (Ps 132:11). Then there was the word given through the prophet Isaiah: "Therefore the Lord himself will give you a sign. Look, the young woman is with child and shall bear a son, and shall name him Immanuel" (Is 7:14). Further on in Isaiah we read about the shoot growing from the stock of Jesse and the flower from his root (Is 11:1). But now we have something more than prophecies, more than signs and figures, to bring us to faith. Truth has come in person, the person of Jesus Christ. He fulfills the whole of the old law and every one of the prophecies of the Old Testament. The gospel story tells us that all is now accomplished, and with the Old Testament texts to confirm it we can be doubly sure that the Lord has indeed saved his people. Now when we look at Abraham, we see that he is truly the father of all nations, because the blessing God promised him is given to the world in Jesus, who is descended from Abraham. Abraham's descendants are not the Jewish people only; all God's adopted children have entered into possession of the heritage prepared for the children of that man who so heroically put his trust in God. This is what St. Paul tells us:

> Hoping against hope, he believed that he would become "the father of many nations," according to what was said, "So numerous shall your descendants

be." He did not weaken in faith when he considered his own body, which was already as good as dead (for he was about a hundred years old), when he considered the barrenness of Sarah's womb. No distrust made him waver concerning the promise of God, but he grew strong in his faith as he gave glory to God, being fully convinced that God was able to do what he had promised. (Rom 4:18-21)

THE LORD TOOK UP ARMS
ON OUR BEHALF

The Son of God waited until the time appointed by his Father and then became man in order to reconcile the whole human race to its Creator. In the beginning the devil deceived the first man and woman and gained a cunning victory over them; it was therefore as man that God decided to overthrow the devil's machinations. He took up arms on our behalf, but they were not the arms of his divine majesty. They were the weapons of our own weakness and our humble, earth-bound condition. He opposed the enemy as one of ourselves, sharing our mortality but free from any share in our sinfulness. He was truly and completely God, and he became a whole and perfect man. He put on our humanity just as God had made it in the beginning before Adam's sin; this was what he undertook to restore in us. There was no trace in him of what the deceiver succeeded in introducing into the garden of Eden, for although he shared our weakness he did not share our faults. He emptied himself and took the form of a slave, but this does not mean that God lost his power. It means that the Creator and Lord of all things was so filled with compassion for us that he stooped down to our level and made himself mortal for our sake. And so when the time came, the Son of God left his heavenly throne and entered the world by the doorway of human birth. Invisible in his own nature, he became visible in ours. Nothing could contain his greatness, yet he allowed himself to be enclosed in his mother's womb. He had existed before time began; now he began a new existence in time. He put a veil over his glory and took on the appearance of a servant. As God he could neither suffer nor die, so he became a man subject to the law of death. The Maker and Lord of all things became one of us.

In the Book of Job we are told that no one is clean from defilement, not even a day-old infant (Jb 14:4), but this does not apply to Christ. A spotless virgin was chosen to be his mother, whom God preserved from all stain. She alone supplied the material for his body, so that even though his birth was miraculous, his humanity was in no way different from ours. But no human father passed on Adam's sin to him. He was conceived in Mary's womb by the overshadowing power of the Holy Spirit. From her he inherited our nature, not our guilt.

The enemy outwitted

Why did the Lord Jesus choose to be born of a virgin? Probably there are a number of reasons. One of them may have been that it was part of his strategy for defeating the devil. Satan was not to know that a savior had been born for the human race. Because of the obscurity of that spiritual conception, he did not see that this child was different from all the rest of humankind. He saw what seemed to be an ordinary baby and thought he had the same origin as any other. Finding the child to be no stranger to any of the weaknesses of mortals, Satan did not realize that he was free from all bondage to sin.

Certainly God had any number of remedies he could have used for our healing. But that particular design for destroying the devil's work put into operation not the force of divine power but the simple dictates of justice. By this I mean that our ancient enemy had been within his strict rights in tyrannizing over people who had of their own accord allowed themselves to become instruments of his will. There would have been no justice in depriving Satan of the time-honored slavery of the human race unless he could be overthrown by one of those he had subjugated.

And so when the Lord Jesus hid the power of his godhead under the veil of our weakness, our crafty foe was taken off his guard. He thought this newborn child who had come to save us was as much his subject as all other humans were. He saw him crying like any other baby; he saw him wrapped in baby clothes, undergoing the customary circumcision and having the offering made for him that the law required. And then he saw him growing up like any normal boy. But, try as he might, Satan could not induce Jesus to commit any sin. It did not matter how many insults, injuries and curses he heaped upon him. He poured out all the force of his fury and exhausted every variety of temptation and test, all without success. He was mystified: he knew that he had effectively poisoned human nature, yet here was a man who was immune to corruption. He had ascertained his mortality by all kinds of proofs, but he was completely unaware that Jesus had no share in the sin of the human race. So he persisted in assaulting him and in exacting from him the penalty incurred by Adam's sin.

But Satan overreached himself. He went beyond the powers he had been granted by requiring punishment from one in whom no fault could be found. And so the terms of the deadly contract were annulled; because of the injustice of overcharging, the whole debt was canceled. The devil was bound by his own chains, and all his evil devices recoiled on his own head.

When the prince of this world was bound, everything he had taken possession of was released. Our humanity was cleansed from its chronic infection and restored to its original dignity. Our death was destroyed by Christ's death, our birth restored by his nativity. We were redeemed from slavery and our race was offered a new beginning. Sin and death were wiped out and humankind set free by the Son of God.

Since no one on earth is free from guilt, everyone qualifies for this liberation. Once we were all castaways, banished from the kingdom of heaven, dying of exhaustion in our exile, reduced to dust and ashes without hope of life. Now through the incarnation of God's Word we have been given the power to return to our Maker, to recognize our true parentage, to shake off the yoke of slavery, to be promoted to sonship. Born of corruptible flesh, we are offered the power to be reborn of the Holy Spirit and to dare to call God our Father.

✚

THE WORD BECAME FLESH

Jesus is the Son of God and Word of God. He was with God from the beginning. All things were made by him, and nothing came into being without him. He did not give up any of his dignity when he took on our ordinariness. He remained God, his glory unimpaired by its alliance with our humanity. His two natures, the divine and the human, preserved their distinct identity, meeting in one person. The majesty of God appeared in human lowliness. The power of God clothed itself in our weakness. The eternal God assumed a body subject to the law of death, that law to which all of us were subject on account of our sins.

God wanted to set us free, and the way he chose was to become one of us. Since his divine nature could not suffer, he united it with one that could. True God and true man were combined in Jesus; he became our go-between, the mediator between God and humankind. Unless he were truly God, he could not save us; unless he were truly man, he could not demonstrate the depth of his love for us. So the Word became flesh. In one nature he would be able to die and by the power of the other he would be able to rise again. In this way he would bring us healing.

Human reasoning and worldly wisdom are useless to us when we try to fathom the mystery of our Lord's incarnation, and if we rely on them we run the risk of denying either the reality of his manhood or his equality with his Father in glory. Nothing but faith can help us here, but that faith is grounded on the authority of God's word: "The Word became flesh and lived among us, we have seen his glory, the glory as of a Father's only son" (Jn 1:14).

The Scriptures, then, teach us that the Son of God took something that was ours without losing anything of his own. Our humanity was renewed in his, but in his divinity he was unchanged and remains forever unchangeable. The godhead which he shared with the Father lost none of its power, nor did the "form of a slave" inflict any damage on the "form of God," because the everlasting being of God which stooped down to save us raised us up to its own glory, never ceasing to be what it had always been. We are sometimes perplexed by those two apparently contradictory sentences of Scripture—in one Jesus says that he is inferior to his Father, and in the other that he is his equal. "The Father is greater than I," he says in John 14:28, and "The Father and I are one," in John 10:30. But these two texts demonstrate the reality of the two natures in Christ. The inequality proves that he was man, and the equality that he was God.

So, then, the human birth of the Son of God took nothing away from his divine glory nor did it add anything to it, because his godhead can be neither diminished nor increased. We say, "The Word became flesh" and have grown used to this expression, but it does not mean that God was changed into a man. It means that the Word of God who is God's own Son took our humanity into his own person, and that he was so inseparably united with it that although he was born of the Father before time began, he was now born in time from a human mother. No other solution was possible to our human dilemma; we could only be set free from eternal death by God becoming humble and weak in our nature and at the same time remaining all-powerful in his own.

A new beginning for humankind

And so our Lord Jesus Christ began a new creation in himself. At his birth he started the spiritual life of the human race afresh. When we are born as human beings we inherit the wound passed on to us by all our ancestors right back to the first man. But in the Lord's plan there was to be a new beginning for humankind; a human being would be born who was not conceived from our sinful human seed, and he would make it possible for the rest of us to be born again "not of blood or of the will of the flesh or of the will of man, but of God" (Jn 1:13).

And we, how can we share in that blessed new beginning? By being reborn in baptism. The water of baptism is like the virgin's womb: it is impregnated by the same Holy Spirit who overshadowed Mary, so that the sin which was destroyed by Jesus' conception may also be washed away by this sacramental cleansing. See then how important it is for us to hold fast to belief in the reality of the Lord's birth from the virgin Mary, because if we do not believe that he was really and truly born, we shall not believe that he really suffered, really died and was buried; and in that case his resurrection will not be a reality and a source of life and power for us.

It is impossible for us to grasp all the implications of this mystery. We can only surrender our mind and tongue to the Spirit and ask him to take them up into praise and thanksgiving for the inexpressible love of our Lord in becoming man for us, changing our guilt into innocence and making our old sin-burdened nature new. We see strangers becoming the adopted children of God and outsiders entering upon the inheritance of sons, sinners beginning to be holy, misers learning to be generous, people in bondage to compulsive vice starting to live clean lives, those who thought of nothing but having a good time on earth thinking about the Lord and about heaven. No one but God could have done this. It is all a gift of his mercy.

Jesus became the Son of Man so that we might become the children of God

Yet we can never sit back and think we are exonerated from taking any part in our own salvation. We have been freed from the devil's tyranny and have renounced his lies, but we still have to keep watch in case he tries to trap us again. Our old enemy never rests, and he can transform himself into an angel of light in his efforts to deceive us and corrupt our faith in the Lord Jesus. He is no fool, and he knows our weak spots. He knows which of us he can tempt with greed for power, who can be enticed into overeating, who can be lured into some other form of self-indulgence or laziness. He knows the most likely person to poison with jealousy and resentment, to overwhelm with grief, to paralyze with fear, to cheat with success, or to bewilder with contradictions. There is no one whose habits he does not study or whose cares and affections he does not weigh up. Wherever he sees a person most engrossed, there he seeks his opportunity to do that person harm. He has plenty of accomplices too, people who he has ensnared so that he can use their talents and their tongues to deceive others. He has his false prophets and his counterfeit spiritual gifts.

But we must recognize the dignity of our human nature. We were made in the image of God, an image which was indeed defaced in Adam, but which has been restored in Christ. Let us always remember whose members we are, what a head we have, who it was that incorporated us into himself, and who it was that we received into our human clan. By being born, the Lord Jesus became one flesh with us. By being reborn, we became one body with him. Anyone who is reborn in Christ, no matter where, leaves the old ways behind and becomes a new person, belonging now to the family of Jesus more than to earthly relatives, because the whole point of Jesus' becoming the Son of Man was to give people power to become the children of God.

However, it is necessary for us constantly to claim our share of Christ's sonship and to renounce the lifestyle of those who are still spiritually dead. God has made us partners in his own divine nature; far be it from us to return to the unworthy servitude of the past! We have been snatched from the power of darkness and taken up into the light and kingdom of God, and by our baptism we have become temples of the Holy Spirit.

The peace of Jesus

Our Savior, then, is born; not as an event of long ago, but born here and now for us who believe in him. He was born of Mary by the power of the Holy Spirit, and by the power of the same Holy Spirit he is born in us. As St. Paul tells us, we have not received the spirit of this world but the Spirit that comes from God, so that we may know the things God has given us (1 Cor 2:12). This means that the only way we can worship God is to offer him the gifts we have ourselves received from him. He has an unfailing treasury of good things, but of all he has given us, the best Christmas present we can offer him in return is the gift of his own peace. It was at Christmas that the angels first proclaimed peace on earth. But what is peace? It is wanting what God wants for us, and not craving for what he forbids. There is no other way to open our hearts to the peace of Jesus. We can never have it if we try to gratify ourselves with what is displeasing to God and to get pleasure from things that are offensive to him. That is not the spirit of the children of God. We are God's family; we must live up to the dignity of our new birth as his children, and love what our Father loves.

What greater blessing could he give us than to call us his children and to encourage us to call him Father! We know that, according to St. John, the world around us is in the power of the evil one (1 Jn 5:19). The devil and his underlings can see the effort we make to rise above our fallen nature and live as God's children, and they are continually attempting to frighten and discourage us by the unpleasant things that happen to us, or to turn our heads by the success and good fortune that come our way. But we have someone living in us who is far stronger than our adversary. If we are at peace with God and if, with all our hearts, we say to the Father at every moment, "Thy will be done," we shall never be overcome. No attack will be able to vanquish us, no assault to hurt us. When we confess our sins and acknowledge our own guilt, when we refuse to give in to the urgings of our lower nature, we stir up against us the hostility of the instigator of all evil; but by freely surrendering our lives to the Lord we secure a peace with God that nothing can destroy. If we claim the gift of his Spirit in order to choose what God wants and to reject what he prohibits, then a wonderful thing happens. We experience his power at work in us, and we find him taking over our struggles and finishing our battles for us. He who gives us the will to serve him gives us also the assurance that he is working with us. Knowing this, we can rejoice in him and sing in triumph: "The LORD is my light and my salvation; / whom shall I fear? / The LORD is the stronghold of my life; / of whom shall I be afraid?" (Ps 27:1).

CHAPTER TWO

The Strong Man Attacked
Epiphany

✠

GOD'S TIMING IS ALWAYS PERFECT

Sometimes we ask ourselves why the Lord makes us wait so long for an answer to our prayers. If his love for us is so great, how is it that he does not heal us straight away when we turn to him for help?

This question has been asked in every generation. It is the universal cry of the human heart, voiced by the psalmist when he complained, "How long, O Lord? Will you forget me forever?" (Ps 13:1), and by the martyrs in the Book of Revelation lying slain beneath the altar (Rv 6:10). But just as Job had to learn how limited was his knowledge of the mind of God, so we too must realize that as high as the heavens are above the earth, so high are the Lord's ways above our ways and the Lord's thoughts above our thoughts (Is 55:9). His vision of our situation includes factors that are hidden from us. We see only our present need, but his eyes range ahead over the whole of our lives, and not of ours only, but of all those other lives which are affected by ours. He sees the deep needs of each one of us and of the whole of humankind.

When God created human beings with freedom to choose whether or not to obey him, he saw what this would lead to. He saw that humankind would misuse this priceless gift and drag the whole world with it into ruin. But because God loved the world so much he made provision even then for its salvation, with a plan that would come into effect when the time was ripe and the human race had tasted the full bitterness of the forbidden fruit. When all nations had turned away from worshipping the true God and even God's chosen people had experienced their failure to keep the law given them through Moses, then the whole human family would be ready for the salvation he had prepared for them in his Son Jesus Christ, and his mercy would have full scope.

God's timing is always perfect. He was neither too soon nor too late. If he had intervened earlier, the world would not have had time to realize how deep was its need, how far gone its disease. If he had not come when he did, the whole of humankind would have perished, for there was no longer any justice left on earth; everyone was given over to the search for empty pleasures and the pursuit of evil. But God chose to take away humanity's sins at a time when no one could boast of merit, so that the world might see the magnitude of his grace.

This was in the days when the legitimate succession of kings in Judea had failed and the power of the Jewish high priests had been suppressed. The throne was occupied by Herod, a non-Jew. However, the coming of the true king had been prophesied long before in the Scriptures. In the Book of Genesis it is written: "The scepter shall not depart from Judah, nor the ruler's staff from between his feet, until tribute comes to him; and the obedience of the peoples is his" (Gn 49:10).

He to whom the scepter belonged was Jesus Christ, the mediator between God and humankind. When he put on the nature which is common to all humanity, he chose to be born in an insignificant little Palestinian town. But it was not his intention to hide the beginning of his earthly life within the shelter of his maternal home or to limit his mission to a small circle of devout Jews. He who had come to save all people wanted to be known by all people. While still an infant, therefore, he revealed himself to men who represented all the nations of the world.

It is this revelation of Jesus Christ, true God and true man, as the Savior of the whole human race that we celebrate on the Feast of the Epiphany.

WHERE IS HE WHO IS BORN TO BE KING OF THE JEWS?

Abraham was the father of the chosen people in the flesh, and from his stock the long-promised king was to come. But his children in the spirit would be all those future generations who would imitate Abraham by putting their faith in God. These were the nations he had been promised as his posterity, the descendants whom God likened to the stars in number. They were summoned to life by the rising of a new star, a star more brilliant than any other in the sky. It was the Lord's plan that this heavenly body should first be seen in the east, among people who knew the art of reading the stars, and be to them a sign of the birth of a child who would rule over Israel. The Holy Spirit inspired the wise men of that country to seek out the child and pay him homage, and so it came about that while the people of the old covenant were still ignorant of the birth of their Messiah, the Lord brought it to the knowledge of the gentiles who would have faith in him.

The wise men would have been familiar with the sacred books and prophecies of their contemporaries, and may have known the ancient oracle of Balaam recorded in the Book of Numbers: "A star shall come out of Jacob, and a scepter shall rise out of Israel; one out of Jacob shall rule" (Nm 24:17). At any rate they set out for Jerusalem, thinking the royal city was the obvious place to find the royal baby. But when they discovered their mistake, they inquired from the Jewish leaders what the Scriptures had to say about the Messiah's birthplace. Through the priests and scribes they heard the Spirit telling them: "You, O Bethlehem, though you are the least of the clans of Judah, from you shall come forth for me one who is to rule in Israel" (Mi 5:2). Strengthened in faith, they took up their journey with renewed eagerness to discover the child whose birth had been revealed by the brilliance of the star and confirmed by the sure word of prophecy.

The first persecution of Christians

Herod, meanwhile, was so racked with fear of losing his throne that he ordered the massacre of all the male children of Bethlehem in an attempt to exterminate his dreaded rival. So the persecution of Christians by unbelievers began at the very birth of our Lord. This first persecution, however, gives us an example of the way in which God is able to use everything, even apparent disasters, to further his merciful plan.

Herod had hoped to rid himself of the threat to his sovereignty by murdering the child in his cradle, thus suppressing the royal pretender before he could gain a following. But the slaughter of a whole town's infant population could scarcely pass unnoticed. While the wise men made their way home to their own country to report what they had seen and heard, the news of the atrocity, along with the tale of the mysterious star announcing the birth of a prince of the house of David, was being rapidly carried throughout the Roman empire. And while King Herod congratulated himself on the death of his rival, the Savior of the world escaped to Egypt. The time had not yet come for him to shed his blood for the world's redemption. The sick had first to be healed, demons cast out, the dead raised to life, and the Good News preached to the poor.

The Lord, then, went down to Egypt, to visit the cradle of the chosen race. Long before, in that very land, Joseph had given bread to his brothers and saved them from famine; now the true Joseph had come who was to give his brothers the bread of life. And in that land where the slaying of the passover lamb first celebrated God's deliverance of his people from bondage to Pharaoh, there entered as a refugee the true Lamb of God who was to be sacrificed for our salvation from bondage to sin and death. The people of the Nile, still living in the darkness of superstition and idolatry, received Incarnate Truth as an unknown guest among them. His hidden presence was a secret grace preparing their hearts to believe the gospel which he was to proclaim to all the nations of the earth.

Already Christ was enlightening the gentiles with the revelation, which the leaders of his own people refused to accept. The scribes indicated the way to the wise men, but would not take it themselves. They opened up the road for others, but closed it for themselves by their own hardness of heart. So it came about that the ignorance of Herod's innocent victims stood them in better stead than the learning of the men he consulted. The scribes were able to point out the town where it had been prophesied that the Messiah would be born and to provide scriptural references in support of their answers, but the children of Bethlehem, while still too young to profess their faith in words, bore witness to Jesus with their blood.

Even before Jesus himself had attained the use of speech, he was exercising the power of the Word and drawing little ones to himself. Already he was saying in effect: "Let the little children come to me, and do not stop them; for it is to such as these that the kingdom of God belongs" (Lk 18:16). The Holy Innocents became the first fruits of Christ's redeeming work, and their lesson to us is that if two-year-olds are capable of the glory of martyrdom, no age or condition is ineligible for entry into the kingdom of heaven.

How easy it ought to have been for the Jewish leaders to believe the lesson they passed on to the wise men! But it seems as though they shared Herod's ideas and expected Christ's kingdom to be on the same level as the kingdoms of this world. In spite of their expert knowledge, they were blinded by unbelief. Their understanding could not rise above the letter of the law; they knew nothing of that covenant which the Holy Spirit had promised to write in humans' hearts. And so the gentiles entered into possession of the Jewish inheritance; in the person of the wise men all nations became members of the family of Abraham, receiving the promised blessing which his natural posterity refused to accept.

THE EVER-BECKONING STAR

The day on which the Savior of the world first appeared to the gentiles is a great day for us. When we celebrate the Feast of the Epiphany we are celebrating the dawning of our own glorious hope. In the initial call of the gentiles we ourselves began to enter upon our eternal heritage. "The Father has enabled you to share in the inheritance of the saints in the light. He has rescued us from the power of darkness and transferred us into the kingdom of his beloved Son" (Col 1:12-13). This was what Isaiah prophesied long before: "The people who walked in darkness have seen a great light; those who lived in a land of deep darkness—on them a light has shined" (Is 9:2b). The psalmist foretold it too when he sang: "All the nations you have made shall come and bow down before you, O Lord, and shall glorify your name" (Ps 86:9), and "God has made known his victory; he has revealed his vindication in the sight of the nations" (Ps 98:2). All these prophecies found their fulfillment when the wise men were called from their far-off land and led by the guiding star to recognize and worship the King of heaven and earth; to this day the same star beckons to us, calling us also to worship him and to respond with all our hearts to his grace inviting us to follow him.

Although the Feast of the Epiphany celebrates an event which took place centuries ago, we are not simply commemorating an episode which has been handed down to us from the past. God gives the same gift to us now. The Gospel records the days when men who had no previous instruction in the Jewish religion came from the east to acknowledge the true God, but we see this same thing happening every time people who have only a worldly kind of knowledge and are far from belief in Jesus are brought out of the darkness of ignorance and called to know the true light. It is the same Spirit who is at work in them; the new light that shines in their hearts comes from the same star which leads them to worship the same newborn King. The gifts the wise men brought to Bethlehem are offered by all who come to Jesus in faith. When we acclaim Christ as King of the universe, we bring him gold from the treasury of our hearts; when we believe the Son of God has become a mortal man like ourselves, we offer myrrh for his embalming; and when we declare that Jesus is equal to the Father in glory, we are burning the incense of our worship before him.

The Church grows stronger through persecution

We can find a counterpart for Herod, too: the devil himself, who once secretly instigated the crimes of that murderous tyrant and to this day continues to imitate him. What tormented Herod then torments Satan still: he sees people coming to know their Savior, his own power daily being brought to nothing by those who accept the Lord, and the true King being worshipped throughout the world. So, like his puppet of old, he prepares schemes, he hatches plots, he foments murders, and he makes use of all who are still subject to him in one way or another. In the person of one of them he is consumed with envy and resentment, in another he acts treacherously, in a third he breaks out into open cruelty. He knows only too well that Jesus, the eternal

King, is invincible, and that his cross has overthrown the power of death itself. Since Satan can achieve nothing against Jesus directly, he uses all his skill to injure those who serve him and to deprive new Christians of the fruits of the Holy Spirit before they have time to reach maturity. He makes some of them swell with pride on account of their intellectual attainments, others he deceives with erroneous opinions, others he so flatters that in their self-righteousness they condemn and persecute everyone else.

No doubt Herod the Great was a paranoiac madman whose mania drove him to insane cruelties. And just as all his acts of violence failed to harm the infant Jesus, so the devil's attacks upon the Church are rendered impotent, and he is brought to nothing by the Lord who has filled those who believe in him with such unconquerable love that they can, in all boldness, say with St. Paul: "Who can separate us from the love of Christ? Will hardship, or distress, or persecution, or famine, or weakness, or peril, or sword? As it is written 'For your sake we are being killed all day long; we are accounted as sheep to be slaughtered.' No, in all these things we are more than conquerors through him who loved us!" (Rom 8:35-37).

There have been periods in the Church's history when kings and armies raged against God's people in outbursts of persecution. Their objective was to suppress the name of Christian altogether, but they had yet to learn that the Church grows stronger through persecution. The example of Christians enduring tortures and martyrdom sowed the seed of faith in those who witnessed it, and even to this day the underground Church is strengthened and purified by the attacks of her enemies. Our circumstances are perhaps less uncomfortable, but we still need to be on our guard against Satan and his agents. If he finds open persecution ineffective, he tries hidden methods. Those whom he cannot break with harsh treatment he attempts to soften and subvert by material pleasures. If he cannot bring about the death of Christians, he attacks their way of life. His aim is to substitute covetousness for fear of confiscation, lust for dread of pain. If a person's spirit cannot be broken by the loss of worldly goods, he tempts that person with an itching palm. His hatred of us has not changed, only his methods. Flattery and cajolery are now his tactics instead of tortures. He stirs up strife, kindles passions, sets tongues wagging and hands grasping, and provides every kind of opportunity for wrongdoing; and in all this his sole aim is to induce those who refuse to worship him on bended knee at least to pay him the homage of sinful lives.

Our security is the knowledge of our weakness

The absence of open assault upon our peace has its own dangers, because no one who does not take a firm stand against evil desires can be secure in the freedom which is the privilege of the sons and daughters of God. We need to know ourselves and our own weak points, because these are the areas where Satan will concentrate his temptations. But our security is this very knowledge of our own weakness, because it prevents our relying on our own strength for protection against our enemies and makes us turn to the Lord for help, to "Christ the power of God and the wisdom of God. For God's foolishness is wiser than human wisdom, and God's weakness is stronger than human strength" (1 Cor 1:24-25).

The folly and the weakness of God were what the wise

men found at the end of their journey. They did not find Jesus casting out demons, raising the dead, giving sight to the blind and speech to the dumb, healing cripples or exercising his divine power in any way. All they found was a baby quietly lying in his mother's arms, too young to speak. Not a single sign of his power was apparent; they witnessed one miracle only, the self-abasement of the Son of God. The Good News that was later to be preached throughout the world was here proclaimed in silence.

The earthly life of Jesus began and ended in persecution. His babyhood was marked by suffering, his passion by nonresistance. He chose to be born as man, and at the hands of men he chose to meet his death.

The all-powerful Son of God saved us by humbling himself. In obedience to his Father he lovingly endured all the sufferings his enemies heaped upon him, and by this means destroyed death and its author. When we think of the trials we ourselves have to endure, we have to admit that they are no more than we deserve. "Who can say, 'I have made my heart clean, I am pure from sin?' (Pr 20:9). "If we say that we have no sin," St. John tells us, "we deceive ourselves, and the truth is not in us" (1 Jn 1:8). There is no one so free from guilt that God's justice can find nothing in him to rebuke, or his mercy nothing to forgive. Surely, then, the Lord's humble endurance must be our model. The wisdom of the Spirit does not consist in eloquent speeches, subtle arguments or brilliant accomplishments, but in sincerely choosing the way of humility which the Lord Jesus chose and followed from his mother's womb to the cross.

CHAPTER THREE

Armed Combat
Lent

✚

THE WAY WE LIVE
AFFECTS THE WHOLE CHURCH

The mystery we commemorate on the Feast of the Epiphany must be an ongoing celebration in our lives; everything about us, our whole way of living, has to manifest the Lord Jesus to the world. And for this to be effective, we are in constant need of renewal. No matter how eager we are to serve the Lord, how careful to avoid sin, we cannot live on this earth without some of its dust clinging to us. We are made in the image of God, but that image needs continual cleansing and polishing if it is not to grow dim. Every day we need to turn to the Lord in repentance, putting off our old nature and its selfish habits (Eph 4:22). But as we draw near to the paschal solemnity, when we shall not be calling to mind any isolated article of our faith but celebrating the whole work of our redemption—the mystery of the Lord's death, resurrection and ascension—God asks for a more earnest purification of our hearts. Easter is especially characterized by the joy of the whole Church in the forgiveness of sins—not only the sins of the newly baptized, but also of those who have long been numbered among the adopted children of God. In baptism we were born again to a new life, but the Lord in his mercy grants us an additional daily renewal to counteract the wear and tear of our perishable human nature.

God our Father has made us his sons and daughters by making us members of his Son's own body. We are not saved on our own; we are saved by being incorporated into Jesus Christ together with everyone who believes in him. This means that the way we live affects the whole Church, just as healthy cells contribute to the vitality of a person's whole body while diseased cells infect or weaken it. God has given us his Holy Spirit to empower us to build one another up in faith, trust and love, so that Jesus may be formed in us as one single body. Truly we need each other, for as long as we are mortal we shall be changeable. One day we may be walking steadily in the Spirit in joy and confidence; another day we shall find our old faults rearing their ugly heads again, and we shall feel we have gone backward instead of forward. It is in these times of weakness and discouragement that we need the joy and confidence of our brothers and sisters who are walking in the strength of the Lord, and on the days when it is we who are advancing we can encourage others not to give up hope. No matter how "Spirit-filled" Christians may be, they can never assume that they have finally arrived; our journey is not over until the day we die, and if our desire for progress and our expectancy flag, we are in danger of falling by the wayside.

At this season Satan is raging with fiercer hatred than ever

The Letter to the Hebrews urges us to rid ourselves of every encumbrance and every sin to which we cling, and to run with determination the race that lies before us, keeping our eyes fixed on Jesus on whom our faith depends from beginning to end (Heb 12:1-2). We are all in this race together, and at the beginning of the lenten season the Lord gives us this word: "At an acceptable time I have listened to you, and on a day of salvation I have helped you" (2 Cor 6:2). Surely there is no more acceptable hour for God to show us favor, no day more suitable for being saved, than these days of preparation for the celebration of Christ's victory over sin and death, when with combined effort the people of God declare war on their sins and lay hold of the power to live according to the Spirit.

Certainly we need to be on our guard all the year round against the enemy of our salvation, never leaving any point exposed to the tempter; but at this season greater wariness and prudence are called for, because Satan is raging against us with fiercer hatred. The reason for this is that these are the days when the power of his ancient hold over humankind is being taken away from him, and countless captives are being rescued from his grasp. Men and women, young and old, boys and girls, are being snatched away from him, born again in the waters of baptism which are the womb of Holy Church. No one is refused on account of sin, because to be born again and put right with God is not something to be earned; it is a free gift. To add to Satan's chagrin, he sees lapsed Christians whom he had previously deceived now returning to the Lord in contrition, washed clean by their tears of repentance and the confession of their sins, reconciled to God and to the community of God's people. He knows, moreover, that in a few weeks' time it will be Good Friday again, the day of the Lord's passion, and on that day he will be crushed all over again by the power of Christ's cross. And after that will come the Easter vigil, when all the members of Christ's body will renew their baptismal vows, renouncing him and all his works with a single triumphant voice.

Lent has always had this twofold character. It is a time when the whole Church purges itself of sin through repentance and self-denial, and it is the traditional season for preparing new members for baptism. As the birth of a new creature draws near, the powers of evil are driven out.

No one is exempt from temptation

In preparation for the paschal solemnity the Church has traditionally imposed on her children the greatest and most binding of fasts, setting aside forty days of severe abstinence in union with the forty days that Jesus fasted in the desert after his baptism in the Jordan. Although the severity of this ancient discipline has been alleviated, the Church still urges us to purify our hearts, to overcome our selfish tendencies, and to ask the Holy Spirit to show us all those areas of our lives that are not yet fully yielded to the lordship of Jesus. For none of us can claim to be wholly surrendered to the Lord yet. Life is too uncertain; no one is exempt from temptation or free from sin. If we are not thrown off our balance by things going badly, we are spoiled by their going too well. There is a trap in affluence and a trap in poverty. The one puffs us up with pride and complacency, the other provokes us to bitterness and envy. Even though health is God's gift, it can make us forget our need of him, just as sickness can make us victims of depression and self-pity. If our minds are given over to earthly and material thoughts, it makes no difference whether we are preoccupied with pleasures or worries. Flabbiness caused by indulgence in food, drink and empty amusements is just as much a threat to our health as the tensions caused by anxiety. The Lord himself warned us that the gate is narrow and the way hard that leads to life (Mt 7:14), and that there are plenty of people who take the easy way that leads to death, but few who tread the path of safety that will bring them to eternal life. Most people are prepared to toil harder for worldly goods than for the service of the Lord. When we are surrounded by so many attractions, it is hard work to keep sin at bay and not to let our resolutions weaken under temptation. Even the things that are necessary for human existence can be a snare to us, absorbing our energy and spiritual vigor to the neglect of the things of God. St. Paul has a word for us on this subject:

> Let even those who have wives be as though they had none, and those who mourn as though they were not mourning, and those who rejoice as though they were not rejoicing, and those who buy as though they had no possessions, and those who deal with the world as though they had no dealings with it. For the present form of this world is passing away. (1 Cor 7:29-31)

This does not mean that we have to be without any kind of feeling or affection. The Lord made us flesh and blood, not dry sticks. But it does mean that we always have to remember that we are pilgrims on the earth. The Lord has given us temporary lodgings here below; we are not to settle down in them permanently. He wants us to be fully human in all our emotions, and yet to rest on God's promises, not on the things of this world.

Of course this needs courage and perseverance, and Lent more than any other season both demands and develops these qualities. We are asked to observe a program of self-discipline. If we stick to it for six weeks we shall have gained a victory over ourselves, but this self conquest will have to be persevered in. Mere fasting from good is worthless unless we also abstain from sin. It would be a poor witness to Christ to undertake great bodily austerities if we did not at the same time control our tongues. We must show ourselves to be God's servants by our purity, patience and kindness, by substituting good habits for bad ones, by forgiving injuries and ignoring hurts. We must train ourselves with the weapons of righteousness both to attack and to defend ourselves, so that whether we are held in honor or disgrace our consciences may be at peace, neither puffed up by praise nor crushed by insults. In every circumstance we must learn to rejoice and give thanks (cf. 2 Cor 6:4-10). No matter how exhausted we are, how many burdens are laid on us or how many misfortunes befall us, we can thank God for everything because we know that all things work together for good for those who love God (Rom 8:28).

✛

OUR ONLY MEANS OF CONQUERING THE ENEMY IS TO CONQUER OURSELVES

In the days of Saul and David, it was when the Israelites fell into sin that the Lord allowed the Philistines to oppress them. In order to regain the ascendancy over their enemies, the people were ordered to fast. The Israelites understood very well that they deserved all they had to endure at the hands of the Philistines because they had neglected God's commands and given themselves over to evil practices. It was no use for them to try to win their freedom by taking up arms; they first had to get rid of their sins. And so they began to discipline themselves and to conquer the desires of the flesh in order to be able to conquer their opponents. When they fasted, their oppressors gave way before them, whereas when they indulged all their appetites the enemy held them in subjection.

It is the same with us today. We have our own struggles and conflicts, and we can win by using the same tactics. The Israelites were attacked by human beings; we are attacked by spiritual enemies. We can conquer by bringing our lives into line with God's will for us; then our enemies will give way before us. It is not their power but our lack of self-discipline that makes them a threat to us, and we shall weaken them by overcoming ourselves.

We must ask God's help in this warfare, because our only means of conquering the enemy is to conquer ourselves. How often we come into conflict with our own lower nature, with those unspiritual, unregenerate attitudes that Scripture calls the flesh! What the flesh wants is opposed to what the spirit wants, and what the spirit wants is opposed to what the flesh wants. If the desires of the flesh are stronger, then our spiritual faculties will be dragged down to the level of our lower nature and will be enslaved where they ought to be masters. But if we are determined to serve the Lord and find our joy in his gifts, if we trample underfoot our instinctive tendency to gratify ourselves and refuse to allow sin to rule in our mortal bodies, then our spirit will be in control and no strategy of the evil one will be able to overthrow us. True peace and freedom can only be ours when the flesh is ruled by the spirit and the spirit is guided by the will of God.

Our struggle is not against flesh and blood
Our enemies are continually on the watch for an opportunity to catch us out, and so we can never afford to relax our guard against them. But it is useful to realize that their snares are likely to be more subtle and crafty during Lent when the Lord's people are making every effort to renounce and atone for past negligence. They know very well that Christians are doing all they can to prepare themselves for the celebration of Easter, and so they direct all their spite toward causing them to fall into new sins instead of turning away from their old ones.

Lent is a time for serving the Lord with greater love and care. It is also a time when we must prepare our souls for a fight against temptations, because the more we try to walk in the Spirit, the more determined will be the attacks of the powers of darkness. But the one who is in us is stronger than the one who is against us, and we know that we are powerful in that strength of his and can count on it absolutely. The Lord Jesus allowed us to be tempted by Satan just as we are, and in conquering temptation he fortified us against the assaults we too have to endure. At the same time he showed us the tactics we must employ. It was not by a great muscular effort that Jesus overcame his adversary, but by taking the Word of God from the Spirit and using it as a sword, as St. Paul tells us to do in our turn (Eph 6:17). It was as man and by using the means available to the rest of men that Jesus conquered the enemy of humankind—not by using his almighty power as God. The way he fought was the way he wants us to fight, so that we too can win the victory.

Of one thing we can be very sure: we cannot exercise a powerful ministry without being tempted and tried. There is no faith that is not put to the test; there is no conquest without opposition, no victory without warfare. This life of ours is surrounded by snares, and we live in the thick of battle. If we want to avoid being deceived, we must keep a sharp lookout. If we want to overcome, we must fight. We find this lesson in the Old Testament: "My child, if you aspire to serve the Lord, prepare yourself for testing" (Sir 2:1). These words were written by one of Israel's wise men who, knowing that the service of the Lord entails many struggles and dangers, forewarned the recruit to put him on his guard against the tempter.

Let us really absorb this teaching and arm ourselves for the contest with full consciousness of what we are up against. St. Paul tells us that our struggle is not against flesh and blood, but against cosmic powers, the rulers of the world of darkness and the superhuman forces of evil in the heavens (Eph 6:12). We have to remember that whenever we try to walk in the Spirit and follow the Spirit's guidance our enemies take it as an attack against them, as indeed it is.

The very fact of our seeking the Lord's promises is a challenge to our foes. It is an old quarrel between us and them: they are tortured by our salvation, because they see God inviting us to claim those very things which they have forfeited. Whenever we are raised up, they are cast down; when we are strengthened, they are weakened. The healing we receive from the Lord is a wound to them. So we just take St. Paul's words to heart when he tells us to stand firm, our minds girded with truth and our feet shod with the readiness to proclaim the Good News of peace. At all times we must carry the shield of faith so that we can extinguish all the burning arrows shot by the evil one; we must accept salvation for a helmet and the word of God as the sword the Spirit gives us (Eph 6:14-17). What mighty weapons the Lord has provided for us! What an impregnable defense we have in being armed by the Lord Jesus himself, who has already defeated the devil and is our unconquered leader in the Christian warfare! Surely we have tremendous grounds for confidence in such armor and can enter bravely into the contest, relying not on ourselves but on the Lord, for it is in him that we are strong.

THE MARK OF TRUE DISCIPLESHIP

Since Lent is the time when the devil is especially furious with Christians, we need to join forces in combating him. As the Spirit of Jesus lives in us all, so the good we do is common to all; love binds us together. Even if our health does not allow us to fast from food and drink, we can always fast from sin and in every possible way show kindness and compassion to our neighbor. Thanks be to God, there is nothing in this world that can ever prevent our choosing to do good. The Lord Jesus told us the mark by which everyone would know we were his disciples: if we loved one another. And St. John tells us again: "Beloved, let us love one another, because love is from God; everyone who loves is born of God and knows God. Whoever does not love does not know God, for God is love" (1 Jn 4:7-8).

These words of Scripture prompt us to examine our hearts carefully to see if they are bearing the fruits of love, those fruits of the Spirit that St. Paul describes in his Letter to the Galatians: love, joy, peace, patience, kindness, generosity, fidelity, gentleness, self-control. If we can find these in our hearts, then we can rest assured that God himself lives in us. But we must always be stretching our hearts to welcome him by the persevering practice of kindness and love. If God is love, then our love must know no bounds, for God is boundless.

Because he wants to see his own goodness reflected in us, God gives us the power to do the things he does and to love the people he loves. And so when we are told to love the Lord with all our heart and all our mind and our neighbor as our self (Mt 22:37, 39), we must lay hold of the love of him who made us, clothing ourselves with it, entering into his plan and his judgment and working with him.

The word "neighbor" must not be restricted to those who are close to us; all people are my neighbors, whether I happen to like them or not, whether they are good or bad. We share the same humanity. The one God fashioned us and gave us life. We all breathe the same air, see the same sky, and enjoy the same days and nights, and the Lord blesses us all with the same generosity. Extending his merciful grace to all people, he asks us to imitate him by loving our enemies and praying for our persecutors, since he who pours out his Holy Spirit upon us changes enemies into brothers, strangers into adopted sons, guilty sinners into men justified in the sight of God; and all this he does so that every knee may bow in heaven, on earth and under the earth, and every tongue confess that Jesus Christ is Lord, to the glory of God the Father (Phil 2:10-11).

When we forgive our neighbor, the Lord forgives us

Since our enemy's malice is likely to be more dangerous than ever at this season, we must be still more alert to the promptings of the Holy Spirit to prepare us for the sacred days when all the mysteries of God's mercy meet together. We need an even greater trust in the Lord's help and guidance, and the confidence that we can do all things in him without whom we can do nothing. We are weak, but he who gives us the desire to do his will also gives us the power to bring our actions into line with it. We must allow the Holy Spirit to penetrate into the innermost recesses of our hearts and reveal to us any lack of harmony, any resentment or selfish ambition that we are harboring. We must let the power of his love drive away any uncleanness and the light of his truth dispel all our self-deception and pride. We must yield our thoughts to calmness, not to anger; our tongues to silence, not to complaints; our hearts to forgiveness, not to the desire for revenge. Our Lord summed all this up for us when he said: "Every plant that my heavenly Father has not planted will be uprooted" (Mt 15:13).

Of course we shall stumble over and over again and fall

many times. The Lord knew this well enough when he called us, but he himself gave us the remedy for our falls when he taught us to say: "And forgive us our debts, as we have also forgiven our debtors" (Mt 6:12). Exposed as we are to so many temptations, it is far more important for us to have our own sins forgiven than to get other people's punished. Anyone who refuses to loose his brother's bonds binds himself all the more relentlessly, because to condemn our brother is to condemn ourselves. We must forgive, even if we feel the offender deserves to be punished, because it is the only way we can pray the Lord's Prayer. Jesus knew how hard this would be for us sometimes; he knew all the excuses we should be tempted to find for refusing to forgive, and this is why he singled out this one petition of the Our Father for special underlining, as if the efficacy of all the others depended on it. "If you forgive others their trespasses," he said, "your heavenly Father will forgive you; but if you will not forgive others, neither will your father forgive your trespasses" (Mt 6:14-15).

Although this business of forgiving others is so demanding and difficult for us, it is at the same time a tremendous joy to know that the Lord uses it to heal our own wounds. How often we need forgiveness ourselves for the innumerable faults we fall into! And here we are given the key to it: when we forgive each other, the Lord forgives us. When we show compassion to others, we ourselves experience the compassion of the Lord.

Sharing God's gifts
The blood of Jesus Christ has washed away all our sins. This forgiveness is God's free gift to us; we can never earn it. But

we can and must show that we have received it by forgiving anyone who has hurt us and showing to others the goodness God has already shown to us. We must be ungrudgingly generous toward our underprivileged or handicapped brothers and sisters. It is only right that we should help others out of the store God has given us, so that we may all thank him together and rejoice in what we share. God allows some of his children to be hungry and poor, homeless and sick, for two reasons: so that he can reward the wretched for their patience, and the merciful for their compassion.

By denying ourselves we shall be able to bring help to the needy and so cause many voices to praise God in thanksgiving. The poor are God's special friends, and if he finds us caring for them he will see his own love reflected in us. Indeed it is only because he lives and loves in us that we can do any good at all. We need never fear to be left with nothing for ourselves if we go on giving, because what we give to the poor we give to Christ, and he who was able to multiply the loaves and fishes as his disciples distributed them is able to multiply not only the material goods we give away but also the time, the strength and the patience we spend in serving him in his friends. Our truest possessions are the things we give to others, because they are stored up for us for all eternity in heaven.

SATAN'S CLEVERNESS IS TURNED TO FOLLY

At the beginning of Lent we hear the gospel account of how, immediately after his baptism, Jesus was driven by the Spirit into the desert where he fasted for forty days and was tempted by the devil.

Truly God as he was, the Lord left us in no doubt about the reality of his manhood by the hunger and exhaustion he experienced after his prolonged fast. We can be sure that Satan missed no sign of this weakness. It delighted him, because it meant that Jesus was as much subject to suffering and death as any other man. However, there was a power in Jesus that Satan feared. He had to find out its source, the extent of its threat to his own treacherous designs, and whether there was any possibility of perverting it to his own ends. So he thought of three crafty ways to test Jesus. "If you are the Son of God," he said, "command these stones to become loaves of bread" (Mt 4:3).

Now Jesus could easily have done this. He was the creator of the stones in the first place, and he had the power, if he chose, to change anything he had made into something else, just as at the wedding in Cana he changed water into wine. But here in the desert it fitted in better with his plan for our salvation to overcome his opponent by the mystery of his self-abasement rather than by the creative power of his divinity. In his defense against the tempter he used a weapon which he bequeathed to all his members, namely the principle that man cannot live on bread alone, but on every word that comes from God's mouth.

Next the devil tried to discover whether the man he saw before him was a man in appearance only, an appearance that concealed his divine nature. If so, he would be able to float through the air at will without coming to any harm. "If you are the Son of God, throw yourself down," he suggested, "for it is written, 'He will command his angels concerning you,' / and 'On their hands they will bear you up, / so that you will not dash your foot against a stone'" (Mt 4:6). Again Jesus resisted the temptation. Preferring to defy the devil with a man's obedience rather than with God's might, he replied, "Again it is written, 'Do not put the Lord your God to the test'" (Mt 4:7).

The devil's third effort was to tempt Jesus to lust for power. Before his eyes he dangled a world empire, on condition that Jesus bowed down in worship to Satan himself. But once more Jesus wielded the sword of the Spirit, retorting: "For it is written, 'Worship the Lord your God, and serve only him'" (Mt 4:10).

So by the Lord's wisdom the devil's cleverness was turned to folly. In spite of all his cunning, he was still ignorant of the real nature and power of Jesus. Because in God's design the enemy of humankind was destined to be bound by his former captive, he was allowed to plunge headlong into the persecution of the one man who had come expressly to die for salvation of the world.

THE TRANSFIGURATION
ON MOUNT TABOR

It was the Lord's intention to reveal his true nature and mission to his apostles. Now by teaching and now by miracles, he gradually enlightened their minds until they were able to grasp that he was both Son of God and Son of Man. To accept one without the other would have done them no good. Both had to be believed and professed, and this is why Jesus asked them point blank one day what they themselves believed him to be. This was Peter's great moment. By means of a revelation from the Father he was able to see beyond the appearance of flesh and blood and to declare: "You are the Messiah, the Son of the living God" (Mt 16:16). Upon this profession of faith the whole Christian Church is established.

There was a danger, however, that once the apostles realized that Jesus was the Son of God they might think our human weakness unworthy of him and consider him incapable of suffering. When in fact he began to tell them all he was to endure in Jerusalem at the hands of the Jewish authorities, how he would be mocked and scourged and crucified and rise again on the third day, Peter was at once ablaze with indignation. It was necessary for the Lord to rebuke him and to teach his followers that they must deny themselves and share their master's suffering. People could only save their lives if they were prepared to lose them for his sake.

Jesus knew this was a hard lesson. He was asking his apostles to rejoice in suffering, not to recoil from the cross or to be ashamed of their master's disgrace. They needed now to be assured that the sufferings of his human nature could not dim his glory as God's Son. And so he took Peter, James and John with him up Mount Tabor and allowed them to witness the power of the godhead irradiating his human body, making his face shine like the sun and his clothes becoming white as snow.

Jesus gave his friends this vision to prevent their faith being shaken by the humiliation he was to undergo. At the same time he laid the foundations of the Church's hope, giving his people a glimpse of what lies in store for them and teaching us all, as members of Christ's body, to look forward to a share in the glory which has already been made visible in our head.

Every day the Father tells us to listen to his beloved Son

Sometimes we ourselves seem to be with the Lord on Mount Tabor. The radiance of his presence is so real to us that we exclaim like Peter: "Lord, it is good for us to be here," and we ask him to let us remain always in rapturous contemplation of his transfigured humanity. Peter wanted to build three shelters on the site, one for Jesus and one each for Moses and Elijah, who, as the representatives of the law and the prophets, had appeared talking with Jesus. But Jesus made no reply, because the world could not be saved except by his death. We too have to learn that although the promise of future happiness stands firm, in this life we need to ask for the power of enduring trials rather than for glory, because it is only if we suffer with Jesus that we shall reign with him.

While the impetuous Peter was still speaking, a cloud overshadowed the three apostles. Out of it came the Father's voice declaring: "This is my Son, the Beloved; with him I am well pleased; listen to him!" (Mt 17:5). Listen to him always: his teaching reveals my love to you, his humble obedience glorifies me. He is the one who was foreshadowed in the law and announced by the prophets. Listen to him; it is he who will redeem the world by his own blood. He will bind the devil in chains and plunder his house, carrying off all his captives. By his death he will cancel the record of your sins and pay all your debt. Is the prospect of your redemption so terrifying? Are you afraid to be set free? Be sure of this: all that your master has chosen to suffer is in full accordance with my perfect plan. Do not let it disturb your faith; because of his death, your own death will hold no terrors.

Now this testimony was not given by the Father for the benefit of the apostles alone. It is addressed to us all every day of our lives. We must always be listening to God's beloved Son, hearing his voice in the Scriptures and in our own hearts, for he is the truth and the life, the power and the wisdom of God himself. He is the Savior of us all, who opens the way to heaven and makes his cross into a stepping stone toward his Father's kingdom. How can we be afraid of the cross by which he has redeemed the world! We may indeed have to suffer like him for the sake of justice and truth, but we can never doubt that his promises will be fulfilled, because we know that it is through labor that we come to rest and through death that we pass to life. If we continue to bear witness by our loving faith to the Lord who shared our human weakness, we shall conquer as he conquered, and all that he promised us we shall surely receive.

CHAPTER FOUR

The Strong Man Bound and Stripped

The Sacred Paschal Triduum

✠

LORD, BY YOUR CROSS AND RESURRECTION YOU HAVE SET US FREE!
YOU ARE THE SAVIOR OF THE WORLD

Every time we celebrate the Eucharist, we are celebrating the freedom and salvation Jesus has won for us and reminding ourselves that during his earthly life "In God Christ was reconciling the world to himself" (2 Cor 5:19). There are no seasons of the year when we cannot rejoice in the gift of our redemption and in the things Jesus has done for us, but when we come to Holy Week and the three great days from Holy Thursday to Easter Sunday that the Church calls the Sacred Paschal Triduum, during which we listen to the gospel accounts of Christ's passion and resurrection as they are read in the liturgy, then, above all, the events they relate are present to us as if we were eyewitnesses of all that took place in Palestine in the days of Pontius Pilate. By faith we are present in the Spirit even though we were not present in the flesh at the time, because true faith has the power to transcend past and future and to lay hold of the truth here and now. There is no time gap for us. The things that broke the hearts of Jesus' disciples long ago move ours today, as we too see him betrayed, arrested, falsely accused, mocked, scourged, condemned and crucified.

This does not mean, however, that we share the disciples' disillusion and depression or their panic in the face of the howling mob. We know that, though momentarily shaken, they were carried forward to an indomitable faith in the Lord's resurrection and ascension, and when we ourselves relive the mystery of his passion we never lose sight of the completed work of our redemption. But it is only when we believe and commit ourselves fully to the lordship of Jesus that we begin to enter into the fullness of understanding what he promised. "When the Spirit of truth comes," he told us, "he will guide you into all the truth" (Jn 16:13). It is not enough for us to know the sequence of events. We need the gift of understanding to know why these things took place, to see how the mighty plan of God was accomplished through the instrumentality of his enemies.

ALL THE ANCIENT TYPES AND FIGURES HAVE BEEN FULFILLED

As we listen to the story of the crucifixion, we can see how everything that was veiled under figures and symbols in the Old Testament is given meaning in the mystery of Christ's cross and the blood he shed for the world's redemption.

God first formed a people for himself at the time of the Exodus, when with a mighty arm and outstretched hand he rescued the sons of Israel from slavery in Egypt. The night before he led them out, the destroying angel passed over the whole land, bringing death to all the firstborn of men and beasts. But the houses of the Israelites were marked by the blood of a lamb offered in sacrifice to the Lord, and so God's people were protected from death and delivered from the hands of the Egyptians. Every year afterward they celebrated their deliverance at the solemn festival of the Passover, which Moses instituted as a perpetual reminder to them of all that the Lord had done.

It was part of God's plan that the enemies of Jesus should at last find their opportunity to get rid of him at the Jewish Passover feast, because everything that had been foretold by means of types and figures had to be fulfilled as clearly as possible. The true Lamb of God had to supersede the passover lamb, and the unique sacrifice of Christ's body and blood had to terminate the long sequence of animal victims. It was through the inspiration of the Holy Spirit that Moses had laid down regulations concerning the slaying of the passover lamb, every detail of which prophesied Christ's sacrificial death on the cross. The time had now come for shadows to make way for substance, for types to retire in the presence of reality, for the ancient ritual to be replaced by a new sacrament, for innumerable animal sacrifices to pass into the one and only sacrifice of Jesus Christ, and for the festival prescribed by the old law to find its meaning in the Easter solemnity of our Lord's death and resurrection. The death of Jesus is the true Passover. Instead of saving a single people from subjection to Pharaoh, his sacrifice delivers a whole world from bondage to the devil.

Here is a tremendous mystery. All the signs and figures

of the past foreshadowed it, beginning with Adam's shepherd son Abel, who, when he offered the Lord the firstborn of his flocks, was murdered by his envious brother Cain. Abel's blood is a type of the blood of Jesus, the Good Shepherd, murdered by his brother Jews. In the story of the flood we see a prefiguring of the baptismal waters that wash away the world's sin, and in Noah's ark the wood of the cross which is the only refuge for humankind. In Abraham, who did not refuse God his beloved son Isaac, we are given an image of the Father who so loved the world that he did not spare his own Son. The Law of Moses prescribed various kinds of sacrifices, ritual ablutions, dietary laws and Sabbath rests, but all of these have now come to an end. There is no further need for the annual slaughter of the passover lamb, because "The law indeed was given through Moses; grace and truth came through Jesus Christ" (Jn 1:17). Types have been fulfilled and can now disappear.

Heralds are no longer needed when the one whose coming they announced has arrived. The reconciliation of the human race, so long awaited, is now offered freely to all. Jesus came not to destroy the law but to fulfill it, and, as he promised, not one point of the law has been left standing, none of its instructions left in force, none of the predictions of the prophets unfulfilled. All have passed over into the new covenant of Christ and the sacraments of the Christian Church. The Jewish rite of circumcision becomes Christian baptism; anointing with chrism becomes the sacrament of confirmation; the consecration of levitical priests makes way for Holy Orders; the profusion of animal sacrifices is superseded by the single offering of Christ's body and blood. The Jerusalem temple is replaced by the Christian

Church, the universal sacrament of salvation. Everything has been accomplished. The New Testament has met the Old, and the shadowy figures of the past are revealed in the clear light of the gospel.

✛

IF THE LORD HAD REFUSED TO BE TAKEN PRISONER, NO ONE WOULD HAVE BEEN SET FREE

By the Holy Spirit's gift, we who hear the reading of the passion are able to believe in it with as deep a faith as though we were seeing all those events with our own eyes. We believe that Jesus is both God and man, not only the Word of God but also a fully human being. He shares his Father's divine nature and his mother's human nature, yet there is no amalgamation of the two. As Almighty God he cannot suffer, but as a humble man he is subject to death as we ourselves are. The whole world is in his keeping, yet he allows himself to be taken prisoner by his enemies. He who is the Son of Justice offers no resistance to injustice; incarnate truth is silent before false testimony. Jesus is still God, but he confirms the authenticity of his human birth by undergoing the most cruel bodily sufferings. Under no compulsion to endure these things, he bore them out of love and pity for us, "coming to us with a nature like our own sinful nature to do away with sin" (Rom 8:3).

When the rabble came to arrest him, he had only to open his mouth and say quietly, "I am he," for the whole crowd to stumble backward in confusion (Jn 18:6). This incident proves that the Lord's power was undiminished. He could not have been arrested against his will. But if he had not allowed himself to be taken captive, no one would have been saved. This is why when Peter loyally sprang to the defense of his master and cut off the ear of the high priest's attendant, Jesus restrained him. Jesus had come to die for us, and the glorious victory he was to win through the cross would only have been deferred and our slavery to the devil prolonged if he had refused to be taken prisoner. And so he healed the servant's ear, restoring with his own hand what he himself had created; then he gave himself up to the will of the powers of darkness.

His purpose was to destroy death and its author by dying himself. A display of divine power and resistance to persecution would have made this impossible. He was not to be turned from his resolve by mockery and insults. As the true Lamb whose slaying had so long been foretold, he was offering himself in sacrifice to God for the world's redemption. The new covenant was being ratified in his blood, and the great High Priest was entering the Holy of Holies through the curtain of his own body to intercede for us with his father. Now was the time of transition from law to gospel, from synagogue to Church. When Jesus bowed his head and breathed forth his spirit, the curtain which screened off the inner sanctuary of the temple was violently torn from top to bottom, a sign to all that everything which the old temple worship represented was now accomplished. The new temple was here, the body of Jesus Christ.

So, then, the Jews had their own way with the Lord Jesus, who by his own choice had entered into our human condition and would claim no protection from his divinity against the blows of his enemies. However, by his endurance he was calmly achieving his own purpose. He used all his opponents' assaults to further his own plan, allowing them to lay their wicked hands upon him. By so doing they brought condemnation on themselves, but they were of service to the redeeming work of Christ—a work of which the scribes, the Pharisees and the high priests were completely unaware. "None of the rulers of this age understand this; for if they had, they would not have crucified the Lord of glory" (1 Cor 2:8).

The powers of darkness overthrown

The devil himself was no less in the dark. He did not realize that by attacking Jesus he was destroying his own power, and that if he had refrained from shedding the Lord's blood he would not have forfeited everything that his primordial deception had gained for him; for when Jesus came to free the human race from the effects of mortal sin, he hid his divine power from the devil and confronted him with our human weakness. The human nature we all share was his also, but it was not damaged as ours is, and because of this he was able to take up the cudgels on behalf of us all. If Satan had understood the plan God had conceived in his great love and mercy, he would surely have aimed at pacifying the Jews instead of stirring up their envy. For fear of losing the power he enjoyed over all the rest, he would have been very careful not to lay a finger on the one man who owed him nothing whatsoever. However, his own malice was his undoing. He exacted a penalty from the Son of God which was to bring healing to all his children. He shed the blood that was to become our ransom and life-giving drink. And so his handiwork was destroyed by his own action.

Satan had inflicted a lethal wound upon the whole

human race at its inception, and none of Adam's posterity could escape his iron rule. So even when he observed one man who apparently possessed greater spiritual power than anyone who had ever lived, he still felt secure in the possession of his time-honored rights. Jesus was a member of the human race, reckoned Satan; therefore, he could not escape the universal law, and Satan could stir up his partisans among the Jewish leaders to get rid of him. The man was obviously a threat to him; he was going about healing people of diseases, casting out demons, even raising the dead. Satan could not afford to leave him undisturbed.

When the ruler of this world launched his attack upon the Son of Man, he had all the resources of a mighty intellect to draw upon. Yet he made one fatal mistake. Insofar as he recognized the human nature in Jesus, he was correct. But he failed to realize his total freedom from sin. The first head of our race and Christ, whom Scripture calls the Second Adam, were alike in their humanity, but not in their achievement. "[F]or as all die in Adam, so all will be made alive in Christ" (1 Cor 15:22). Through the pride and covetousness of the first, sorrow appeared on the human scene; through the self-abasement and freely accepted suffering of the second, joy and glory were prepared for us.

And so, unresisting, Jesus held fast to patience. Restraining his legions of angels, he drained the cup of pain and death. By his endurance he transformed his crucifixion into a triumphant victory. Falsehood was overthrown, the powers of darkness subjugated, and the world given a new source of life. No longer would a person's natural birth from the stock of Adam condemn him or her to everlasting death, since he or she could now be saved by being born a second time. "So if anyone is in Christ, there is a new creation: everything old has passed away; see, everything has become new!" (2 Cor 5:17).

THE LORD HAS SHARED OUR FEARS

Yes, indeed, Christ in God was reconciling the world to himself. God put on the nature of one of his own creatures so that he could restore it to the likeness of its Creator. This meant sharing our weakness and our fear of pain by enduring it himself. Jesus trembled with fear in the garden of Gethsemane; he was so afraid that he sweated blood, and he made no attempt to conceal it. But because as man he plumbed the depths of our human fear, he was able to clothe our weakness with the fullness of his divine strength. Like a rich merchant from heaven, he had come into our world to trade with us by giving us his own goods in exchange for what we had to offer: honor for insults, salvation for pain, life for death. Thousands of angels could have rallied to his support and wiped out his enemies, but he preferred the experience of our fears to the exercise of his mighty power.

This was the way the Lord chose to save us, the way he saw in his wisdom to be the best. The first to understand it was Peter, the apostle who had panicked in the face of the mob that came to arrest his master and who had denied him like a coward, frightened by a mere serving girl. It was because the Lord had himself been afraid first that Peter was able to repent of his cowardice and be restored to the rock-like firmness of a true member of Christ's body. Unless death's divine conqueror had been afraid, Peter could never have conquered his human fears. But as he stood quaking in the courtyard of the high priest amid the slanders of the priests, the lies of false witnesses, the blows and the spitting, Peter's frightened eyes were met by the eyes that had foreseen his terror. At that moment the Lord looked upon him with a gaze that penetrated his very heart. It was as if Jesus said to him: "Do not be afraid. This is the time of my ordeal; yours has not yet come. You, too, will overcome. I know your weakness from the inside; I was afraid for your sake. Do not be ashamed of your fears, for I have shared them. Have confidence in me; you, too, will overcome."

WHEN I AM LIFTED UP FROM THE EARTH

"When I am lifted up from the earth, I will draw all people to myself," Jesus prophesied before his passion (Jn 12:32). I will champion every person's cause, I will bear the whole burden of human guilt, I will restore fallen human nature to its original integrity. In me all sickness will be cured and all wounds healed.

Jesus did indeed draw all things to himself when he was lifted up above the earth. As the Creator of all things hung upon the cross, the whole of creation was pierced by the nails and groaned with him in agony. The suffering Christ drew heaven and earth into communion with his pain; rocks split asunder, graves burst open, the underworld gave up its dead, thick darkness shrouded the sun. Thus the earth gave its testimony: how could created things endure when their creator had perished? In protest against his murder everything was thrown into disorder, darkness and confusion, a state which signified and reflected the blindness and confusion of the Jews. They had cried out: "His blood be on us and on our children" (Mt 27:25), and by these words they had called down their own punishment.

Yet Jesus was filled with such compassion for his murderers that even when they were hammering in the nails he prayed not for their punishment but for their pardon. "Father, forgive them," he pleaded, "for they do not know what they are doing" (Lk 23:34). Do you think the Father was deaf to such a prayer? No. Remember the day of Pentecost, when at Peter's words three thousand Jews were converted and baptized. Through the prayer of Jesus his blood was indeed upon them, cleansing, forgiving, transforming, so that they became one in heart and soul, ready now to die for the Lord whose crucifixion they had only recently been clamoring for.

The power of Christ's blood

Yes, the ransoming power of that innocent blood shed for sinners was so great that if everyone had believed in his Redeemer not a single person would have remained in bondage to the devil. "Where sin increased, grace abounded all the more" (Rom 5:20). Those who had been born under a pre-existing law of sin received the power to be born again into a right relationship with God, together with a grant of freedom which invalidated the debt that had held them fast.

But unless a person believes in Jesus Christ, true God and true man, and accepts him as his own Savior, the salvation that is offered to the whole of humankind will be of no avail to him. There have been many good people whose death was precious in the sight of the Lord (Ps 116:15), but never one whose blood was the ransom and propitiation for the whole world. Good men may indeed receive crowns; they cannot bestow them on others. The endurance of Christians may give the world an example of patience, but not the gift of being restored to God's friendship. Each person's death stands alone; no one can pay another's ransom. Only in the Lord Jesus were all Christians crucified. In him we all died and were buried and raised to life again. Because he shared our humanity, we were admitted to God's pardon and peace and given the right to glory in the power of our Savior who wrestled with our insolent enemy in the weakness of our own flesh, and so made over his victory to those in whose flesh he had gained it.

DEATH HAS NO MORE HOLD OVER US

When we look at the cross of Christ with the eyes of faith and realize all it has achieved, we understand why the Church celebrates the Lord's Passover with such solemnity. By the cross Jesus has broken down barriers, healed the divisions of people's hearts and reconciled the world to God.

But we are celebrating Easter in vain unless we are firmly convinced that what we see hanging on the cross is our own human flesh, and that in Jesus, as the first fruits, the whole human race has already been raised to life. It was our human flesh that lay dead in the tomb, our human flesh that rose again on the third day, and our human flesh that ascended above the heavens to the Father's right hand. Jesus had only one aim in all that he did and suffered: our salvation. His purpose was to communicate to the members of his body the power that belongs to him as head. And so, through his grace, the resurrection our bodies will experience in the future is a reality in our hearts even now. The only man who is excluded from the mercy shown to the human race is the unbeliever. Whoever accepts Jesus, the incarnate Word of God, as his Lord and Savior, and is born again of the same Spirit by which Jesus himself was conceived in Mary's womb, receives a share in his divine nature. Yet when we look at this man suffering from hunger and weariness, a man who was troubled and sorrowful and could be moved to tears, we recognize our own humanity crying out for healing and forgiveness. We see once more that when he became the Son of Man, God's only Son lacked no quality belonging to our manhood, nor did he lose the fullness of his godhead.

The great mystery of the incarnation is that true man is in the God whom no suffering can touch, and the true God is in the human flesh that is subject to pain and sorrow. By this wonderful exchange humankind gains glory through shame, immortality through chastisement, life through death. For unless the Word of God were so firmly joined to our flesh that the two natures could not be parted even in death, we mortals would never be able to return to life. But when the Lord became man and died for our sake, death lost its everlasting hold over us; through the nature that was undying in Jesus Christ, the nature that was mortal was raised to life.

Unless a person takes up his cross and follows me, he cannot be my disciple

In our celebration of Easter we must stand firmly on this faith, committing ourselves wholly to the Lord who died and rose again for us. Easter to us does not mean a superficial rejoicing; it calls for our response at every level; for to take part in the paschal mystery is to be numbered among those who share the Lord's passion. We do not really honor the Lord who suffered, died and was raised to life unless we suffer, die and rise with him. This suffering, dying and rising with Jesus began at our baptism, when we died to sin and were born to new life. However, that was only the beginning: what was effected sacramentally has to be carried out in our daily life. We have been born of the Holy Spirit; we must now walk in the Spirit. The life of Jesus is our life now, and this life includes taking up the cross and following him. The tyrant who used to rule over this world has been deprived of his spoils and expelled through the power of the cross from all whom the Lord Jesus has ransomed, yet he still plots against the Lord's people and persists in attacking those who do not conform to his standards. If he finds a Christian negligent, he seizes his chance to drag that Christian away from the community of the redeemed, bringing him or her to partnership with himself in condemnation. Not only does he try to ensnare Christians by temptations to sins of the flesh or to vainglory, but he seeks to sow the seeds of false teaching among the good seeds of the true faith. If he cannot corrupt a person's morals he will poison his or her mind.

So we must be on our guard against his suggestions. We cannot afford to be careless. As soon as we find our old selfish desires leading us astray, we must nail them to the Lord's cross. That cross is our glory; by means of it the world is dead to us and we are dead to the world (Gal 6:14). There on the cross Christ has lifted us up with himself, and there, where the human race was saved, we too must be found. The Lord's passion is not over and done with: it will continue until the end of the world. Just as in the saints it is Jesus who is honored; in the poor, Jesus who is fed and clothed. So in all who suffer for doing right, it is Jesus who suffers. Those who are imprisoned, tortured and executed for their faith are not alone in being called to take up the cross. St. Paul says that all who are resolved to live a holy life in union with Christ Jesus will be persecuted (2 Tm 3:12), and this means that it is only lukewarm Christians who are never tempted. The only people who can have peace with the world of ambition and irreligion are those who love it. There can be no peace or concord between good and evil, lies and truth, darkness and light. The grace of our loving Father is continually drawing sinners to repentance and conversion, while the evil spirits are continually attacking believers, either by subtle craft or by open warfare. Everything right and holy is offensive to sinners. Of course they are only free to do as much as God permits, but they are so skilled in deceiving people and persuading them that they are able to harm or spare their victims at their own good pleasure, so that many people are fooled and become terrified of falling foul to them.

Yet the friendship of evil spirits is more dangerous than their enmity. Their favors hurt us more than their wounds. Jesus is the Lord, the only master whose displeasure Christians need to fear. If we have nailed our sinful desires to the cross, laid down at our Savior's feet any resentments or bitterness that may have been in our hearts, learned to forgive our enemies and to prefer God's will to our own, refused to give in to the urges of our lower nature, and walked in the way of God's Holy Spirit, we have no need either to dread the evil one or to try to appease him. Satan will try to persuade us that the Lord's promise is not true, that God's call is not for us. But Satan has been a liar from the beginning. Jesus has set us free once and for all from his accusations; we have turned over our lives to Jesus and he has given us his Spirit together with the power to endure all the trials of his life with the joy that comes from believing in God's word: "If we have died with him, we will also live with him; if we endure, we will also reign with him" (2 Tm 2:11-12). "If we share his sufferings, we shall also share his glory" (Rom 8:17).

In the power of the Spirit we share Christ's victory

This promise is not confined to the martyrs who bore terrible torments for the name of Christ. The whole community of God's people has been crucified with Jesus and will be glorified with him. Certainly those who have endured persecution with heroic faith and love of their Lord will shine out more brightly than anyone else, but the promised glory is for all God's servants who conquer avarice, pride and vice by putting their selfish instincts to death. Anyone who loves the Lord and tries to live for him is bound to experience the pull of the old Adam as well as the assaults of the devil. But even now Christ is overcoming the world. When his people conquer temptations, it is he who conquers; his is the power and his is the victory. For us Jesus Christ on the cross is neither a stumbling block, as he was to the Jews, nor foolishness, as he was to the Greeks; he is the power and wisdom of God. We are the spiritual heirs of Abraham, not in the line of natural descent but in the Spirit of freedom in which we have been reborn. We have been delivered from slavery under Pharaoh by the mighty hand and outstretched arm of the Lord Jesus who has been offered in sacrifice for us as the true Lamb without blemish.

Praise our God for this wonderful victory, this great passover sacrifice of our salvation! Let us make haste to be renewed in the likeness of our Lord, who made himself like us in our deformity; let us reach out to him who turned our miserable clay into his glorified body, and walk in his humble and patient footsteps so that we may claim a share in his resurrection. By the Lord's great mercy we have been healed and set free; we must guard our healing and our freedom. It is not something we have achieved ourselves, but God's free gift to us, and Scripture warns us not to treat God's gifts carelessly. The Lord has saved us, but we have to hold fast to our salvation by walking in the way he has mapped out for us.

Jesus himself is our way, as he told his disciples when he said: "I am the way, and the truth, and the life" (Jn 14:6). We come to the Father along the road of his Son's endurance and humiliation. On that road we shall encounter toil and heat, fear and distress. The unscrupulous will lay snares for us, unbelievers will try to stop us, we shall be mocked, threatened and insulted. All these things were endured by the Lord Jesus; he passed through them in our fragile and vulnerable flesh on his way to glory. St. Peter says: "Christ also suffered for you, leaving you an example, so that you should follow in his steps" (1 Pt 2:21). Jesus conquered through all these trials, and his lesson to us is not to try to avoid them, but to overcome them in the power of his Spirit.

CHAPTER FIVE

The Plunder Divided
Easter to Pentecost

✠

YOU HAVE BEEN RAISED TO LIFE WITH CHRIST

It was Christ's will that his body should be mortal up to the
time of his resurrection, so that we who believe in him
might know for certain that, as his members, we too can be
victorious over suffering and death. We share his divine
nature, and therefore we also share his victory and glory. All
of us who believe in Christ and are born again in the Holy
Spirit form a single community in Christ's sufferings and in
his risen life. We do not celebrate the paschal mystery with
the old yeast of sin and wickedness, but with the unleav-
ened bread of purity and truth (1 Cor 5:8), no longer living
as members of the first Adam but as members of the body of
Christ. If we really believe in our hearts what we profess
with our lips, then not only has Christ died and been raised
to life for us, but in him we too have been crucified, in him
we have died and have been buried, and on the third day we
have been raised to life again. St. Paul explains this clearly to
the Colossians. "When you were buried with him in baptism,"

he said, "you were also raised with him *through faith in the active power of God* who raised him from the dead" (Col 2:12, emphasis added). And since we have a new life, St. Paul goes on to tell us how we must live from now on. "So if you have been raised with Christ, seek the things that are above, where Christ is seated at the right hand of God. Set your minds on things that are above, not on things that are on earth, for you have died, and your life is hidden with Christ in God. When Christ, who is your life revealed, then you also will be revealed with him in glory" (Col 3:1-4).

The Lord knows how impossible it is for us to set our inconstant hearts on the things that are in heaven, or to keep our minds fixed on things there rather than on things here below. We can only do it if he himself lives in us by his Spirit. However, we have his solemn pledge in the Gospel: "Remember, I am with you always, to the end of the age" (Mt 28:20). It is a promise contained in the very name he was given by the prophet Isaiah: Immanuel, God-with-us. Jesus is true to his name; though he has ascended to heaven, he has not forsaken his adopted brothers and sisters on earth. He is with us still. He who has taken his place at the Father's side is the same Lord who is the head of that body of which we are all members. In him we find strength to endure suffering here on earth, and in him we shall receive our share of glory in heaven.

With a promise like this, what need is there either to seek empty pleasures apart from the Lord or to give way to cowardice under trials? There will be plenty of pressures from the world to entice us, and there will be plenty of hardships to endure, but the earth is full of the Lord's mercy. Wherever we are, Christ's victory is always available to us.

"But take courage," he told his disciples, "I have conquered the world" (Jn 16:33). He speaks the same word of life to each of his members today, telling us not to fear because he who has conquered the powers of darkness is alive in us as the light of the world. It is always Easter for us as long as we hold fast to our faith in him and reject all attachment to sin.

✠

CHRIST, OUR PASSOVER, HAS BEEN SACRIFICED

In Genesis we read about the cherub with the flaming sword who was posted at the entrance of the Garden of Eden to keep Adam and Eve from taking the fruit of the tree of life (Gn 3:24). Until Christ's precious blood quenched the flames of that sword, humans were shut out of their heavenly country. But now the Lord's people are invited to enter into paradise and enjoy its treasures. Everyone who is reborn is able to return to the lost country by taking the road which Jesus has opened up, a road which can only be closed to people in the future through their own fault.

Once we were ignorant of God; our lives were dark and despairing. But in his great mercy we have now been adopted as God's children and incorporated into the people whom he chose long ago. Our present task is to shake off our lethargy and reach out for the gifts he has promised us. When we think of the wretched state of bondage from which the Lord has rescued us, the price he paid for our salvation and the mighty power with which he set us free, our response can only be to praise and worship him with all our hearts and to glorify him who has given us a share in his own risen life. Our whole lives from now on should bear witness to him. People should be able to see that he lives in us by the way we live. "See how these Christians love one another" is still the mark by which we testify to the risen Lord—this, and our freedom from worldly ambition and sinful habits. Loving service and shining purity are like two wings by which the Lord can raise us up from earth to heaven. But we have to seek these wings from him and ask for them in faith, recognizing that they are his gift, that his Spirit alone is the wind that empowers them, and that the glory is all his.

By faith we enter into the secret of the Easter mystery. The destroying angel cannot cross our threshold, because our doorposts are marked with the blood of the Lamb and the sign of the cross. We need not fear the plagues of Egypt; we have seen our enemies drown in the waters by which we ourselves have been saved. Christ, our Passover, has been sacrificed. Our bodies and souls have been cleansed and purified; if we follow the guidance of the Holy Spirit, no temptation will be able to separate us from the love of Christ who has brought peace to the whole world by his blood, and who, in returning to his glorious home at the Father's side, has not forsaken his humble servants here on earth.

Now that the Lord has done this wonderful thing for us, we can no longer live for ourselves. Our lives must be wholly given over to him who died for us and rose again (2 Cor 5:15). Our old life is behind us; we are given a new life as members of Christ's risen body. But this life still has to grow; it cannot be stationary. Anyone who is not moving forward is bound to slip back. If we are not gaining ground we are losing it. Not only must we walk in the Spirit, we must run toward the Lord in faith and trust, celebrating the day of our redemption always in our hearts, his life within us bearing fruit in service and love.

What a price the Lord has paid for us, how tremendous the mystery by which we have been snatched from the powers of darkness! We must take every care not to let the old enemy deceive us again. Satan will do his best to prevent our receiving the eternal life Jesus has won for us, but we must be quite clear from the outset about the source of any doubts arising in our minds against the Christian faith, any suggestions contrary to God's commandments. They are the devil's efforts to bring us into captivity once more. All of us, then, who have been born again in water and the Holy Spirit, must remember the promises we made at our baptism and renewed on Easter night: we solemnly renounced Satan and threw off his yoke, and gave our whole lives to the Lord.

WE ARE ALREADY IN POSSESSION OF WHAT WE BELIEVE

During Lent our aim was to experience some share in the sufferings of the cross and to enter into the mystery of the Lord's passion by taking up our cross and following him along the way of his humiliation and endurance. Now, during Eastertide, the accent is on sharing his resurrection. Not for any merit of our own, but through the blood of Christ and the free gift of God's grace, we have been healed and set free. What the Lord asks of us now is not to try to earn this freedom, but to hold fast to what he has already given us and to guard it from the devil's envy. In the Lord Jesus we have passed over from death to life, but while we are still on earth his Passover must be continually renewed in us. We have to be dead to Satan and alive to God; we have to abandon sin in order to rise to holiness. Jesus himself said: "No slave can serve two masters" (Lk 16:13). Our business is to make sure that the master we serve is the Lord who has raised up fallen people to glory, not the one who brought upright people to ruin.

St. Paul tells us that "the first man was from the earth, a man of dust; the second man is from heaven. As was the man of dust, so are those who are of the dust; and as is the man of heaven, so are those who are of heaven. Just as we have been the image of the man of dust, so we will also bear the image of the man of heaven" (1 Cor 15:47-49).

Praise God for this wonderful exchange, by which we are transferred from earthly disrepute to heavenly honor! In his great mercy the Lord descended to our level in order to lift us up to his, by taking on himself not only our human weakness but also our sins, and allowing himself, God though he was, to be assailed by all the sufferings which are the lot of mortal humans.

It was his will to die for us, but death could not keep him. The body that was laid in the tomb and the soul that descended to the world of the departed were the body and soul of the Son of God. Through his own will they were separated when he bowed his head on the cross and gave up his spirit; through his divine power they were reunited on the third day. The Gospels tell us of the rolling away of the stone, the empty tomb, the linen cloths, the angel witnesses, and the Lord's appearances to the women and to the apostles. All this evidence formed the basis for the preaching of the faith throughout the whole world. Not only did Jesus speak with his disciples, but he ate with them, allowing them to touch him and to probe his wounds. He entered the upper room where the doors were shut and greeted them with the words "Peace be with you"—peace to quiet their troubled hearts and to assure them of the unfailing constancy of his love and forgiveness. To bring God's love and forgiveness to the world had been his mission from the Father; now he passed on that mission to his apostles. "As the Father has sent me," he told them, "so I send you. Receive the Holy Spirit. If you forgive the sins of any, they are forgiven them; if you retain the sins of any, they are retained" (Jn 20:21-23). Patiently he went through the Scriptures with them to show them everything that had been written about him in the Old Testament, how it had been ordained from the beginning that the Messiah should suffer and so enter into his glory. After this he showed them the wound in his side and the marks of the nails. By his own choice he had retained these scars in his body in order to heal the wounds of their unbelieving minds. Now they knew with absolute certainty that the risen body, radiantly alive in their midst, was the same body that had been born in Bethlehem and had suffered on the cross. From now on it would be seated with God the Father on his heavenly throne.

But after the resurrection Jesus' body possessed a new quality, a new mode of being. Before Calvary it had been vulnerable, capable of suffering and death; now it was immune to pain, immortal and incorruptible. And in his glorified flesh we see the beginning of what we ourselves have been promised. Since we have been incorporated into him we are not, as it were, hanging in suspense, wondering if we shall win through to our own resurrection; instead we rejoice and thank God for the elevation of our own human nature in Jesus, because we are already in possession of what we believe.

Our resurrection has already begun

To share Christ's resurrection means not to be shackled by temporal things but to set our hearts on the eternal life he is offering us here and now. It is true that at present we are only saved "by hope" (Rom 8:24). Our flesh is still mortal and corruptible as long as we are on this earth, yet we can stop living "according to the flesh" if we refuse to allow our natural appetites to rule us. St. Paul tells us to "make no provision for the flesh, to gratify its desires" (Rom 13:14). By this he does not mean that we have to deny our bodies what their health and well-being require. "No one ever hates his own body" (Eph 5:29). But we must now take care of our bodies for the sake of serving the Lord, not for the sake of indulging ourselves. We are a new creation in Christ Jesus, and we must at all times be clear in our minds who it is who has made our nature his own and who has given us a share in his nature. Christ has made us his members, and we have acknowledged him as our Lord and Savior. Now that we have begun to live a new life in him, let us take care not to return to our former useless existence. We have put our hands to the plow; we must not give up or look nostalgically at what we have left behind, but keep our attention on what we are sowing. It would be the greatest tragedy to fall back again into the hopelessness from which the Lord Jesus has raised us up. We may still be afflicted with bodily infirmities, but we believe that the Lord has taken all our diseases upon himself in order to heal us, and therefore we can pray in faith and trust to be made whole. "By his wounds you *have been* healed," (1 Pt 2:24, emphasis added). It is a fact: our resurrection has already begun in Christ, and he longs to lead us into the fullness of life and healing. No doubt we shall have many accidents and falls during this slippery life on earth, but "Our steps are made firm by the LORD, / when he delights in our way; / though we stumble, we shall not fall headlong, / for the LORD holds us by the hand" (Ps 37:23-24). God is continually guiding our feet out of the quagmire of preoccupation with present circumstances to the solid ground of joy and thanksgiving in the eternal life of heaven, helping us to rise again from our falls and to press forward to the fullness of the resurrection, when our bodies too will be glorified with Christ Jesus our Lord.

✠

GOD ALLOWED THE APOSTLES TO DOUBT SO THAT WE MIGHT BELIEVE

The forty days Jesus spent in the desert before he began his public ministry were a period of preparation for his task of proclaiming the kingdom of God to the people of Israel. After his resurrection he spent another forty days preparing his apostles for their task of preaching the Good News to the whole world. Throughout this time his bodily presence remained with them, visible and tangible, in order that their faith in his resurrection might be strengthened by the evidence of their senses.

The truth is that in spite of all the warnings he had given

them, Christ's death had seriously disturbed the hearts of his disciples. They were crushed with grief at the agony of his crucifixion, the horror of his death and the sight of his mangled body as it was taken down from the cross and hastily laid in the grave. When the women came running to them in the early hours of the first morning after the Sabbath with the news of their expedition to the tomb, the discovery of the stone rolled away from the entrance, the body missing and the two men in shining white telling them Jesus had risen, the disciples could not take it in. They were in a state of shock, their minds numb and incapable of grasping the hope held out to them, and they dismissed the tale as nonsense.

Was this shattered, skeptical group to be the foundation of the Lord's Church? Were these weak and broken men to convert the whole world by their testimony? We may ask how the promised Spirit of Truth could have allowed his future preachers to be engulfed by such doubts. But, as always, it was part of God's perfect plan. He intended their fears and hesitation to lay the foundations of our own belief. It was against our crises of faith that the Holy Spirit made provision in the apostles, ourselves in those men who were taught how to meet the accusations of unbelievers and the arguments of worldly wisdom. Because they saw Jesus, our minds are enlightened; because they heard him, we are convinced; because they touched him, our faith is confirmed. Thanks be to God for that scrupulous caution on their part! Because God allowed them to doubt, we are able to believe without wavering.

It was on the evening of Easter Sunday that the Lord Jesus joined two of his disciples as they trudged home to Emmaus after the traumatic events of his betrayal and execution.

Walking along the road in their company, he gently chided them for their timidity and reluctance to believe, and by so doing he swept away the mists of our own uncertainty. As he explained the Scriptures to them, their lukewarm hearts were set on fire and began to burn within them; as they shared their meal with him, their eyes were opened in the breaking of bread. They knew him as their risen Lord. In their very presence they saw their own humanity glorified in the man Christ Jesus.

How wonderful must have been that moment of recognition in contrast to the shame our first parents felt on the day their eyes were opened to realize their sin! How often we have wished we could have been there to share that wonderful experience and to listen to Jesus' explanation of the scriptural texts! But he promised the night before he was betrayed that the Holy Spirit would bring back to the minds of his disciples everything he had said to them, and this promise of his abides forever with the Church. When in the liturgy we hear the great texts of the Old Testament, which predicted all that the Christ was to suffer, and listen to the gospel accounts that reveal how these promises were fulfilled, out hearts too begin to burn within us as the Lord opens up the Scriptures to us. And as the Church celebrates the Eucharist which he left to her as a memorial of his blessed passion, resurrection and ascension, we too know the Lord Jesus in the breaking of bread.

The period between Christ's resurrection and ascension was by no means uneventful, for it was the time when the great truths of our redemption were made clear to the apostles. The way in which the power of Christ's saving work becomes available to believers through the sacraments was revealed, and what we refer to as the "deposit of faith" was completed. The Lord left nothing undone; he made careful provision for the ministry of Word and Eucharist, establishing his Church on the foundation of this specially chosen group of men and entrusting to Peter the care of his whole flock.

Those were the days when death lost its terrors for the apostles, who now knew that both body and soul can live forever. The Holy Spirit had at last convinced them that Jesus, who was truly born, truly suffered and truly died, was truly risen from the dead. Now they were ready to turn to the task of preaching the Good News throughout the world. So strengthened were they by the evidence of the Lord's resurrection that when the forty-day period came to an end and he left them to return to his Father, they were filled with immense joy and thanksgiving.

The Lord's ascension is our own elevation

We might be excused for expecting the disciples to have felt sad and disconsolate at the ascension of their beloved master, who had apparently returned from the dead only to leave them once more. But their faith in his promises was now so sure that when they saw him entering heaven in the triumph of his victory over death, they experienced nothing but pure joy. "If you loved me," Jesus had told them, "you would rejoice that I am going to the Father, because the Father is greater than I" (Jn 14:28). If we had only this saying of our Lord, we might decide that he was not truly God. But he had also said: "The Father and I are one" (Jn 10:30), and "Whoever has seen me has seen the Father" (Jn 14:9), and so we are able to accept the first statement without concluding that it implies any essential difference within the godhead. What the Lord wanted the apostles to understand was that it was humankind who was promoted when the Word became flesh. "If you loved me," he said, "you would rejoice that I am going to the Father." In other words, if only you realized how much you gained when God's only Son was born of a human mother, when the eternal Lord chose to become a mortal man, when the invisible God appeared in visible form and took the nature of a slave, you would indeed be glad that I am going to the Father. This ascension of mine is a free gift to you; it is your lowly existence that is raised up in me to the Father's right hand. You can truly rejoice, then, that I am going to the Father who is greater than I, because when I go, you go with me as my members, the people I have made one with myself. I became the Son of Man so that you could become the children of God. As a man like yourselves I am less than the Father; as God I am his equal. So let what is less than the Father go to the Father; where the Word has always been, there let the flesh find an everlasting home.

The Lord's ascension is indeed our own elevation. We who are his body are continually called by the Spirit to raise our hopes to our Father's house, where Jesus our head has made his glorious entry before us. Not only are we confirmed in the possession of paradise, but in Christ we have already penetrated the innermost sanctuary of heaven and have gained far more through his free gift than we had lost through the devil's envy. In his malice the enemy robbed the human race of the happiness of its first home, but the Son of God has taken us into himself, making us members of his own body and setting us at the right hand of his Father. This is the day when our poor, weak human nature is carried up in Christ above all created spirits, above all the ranks of angels, beyond the highest heavenly powers to the throne of God himself. To that human nature in Adam it was once said: "You are dust, and to dust you shall return" (Gn 3:19); to that same nature in Christ it is said today: "Sit at my right hand" (Ps 110:1).

✣

Our Redeemer has not left us orphans

Jesus has finished the work his Father gave him to do, the work of our salvation which was so precious in his eyes that he valued it at the price of his own blood. All the stages of his earthly life from his birth through the hidden years and public ministry to the time of his passion, death, resurrection and ascension form a harmonious structure upon which we have been firmly established, so that in spite of his withdrawal from human sight we still hold fast to faith in him. We do not need to see him in order to give him all our love and trust. When people truly believe, they put their faith in what their eyes cannot see and fix their hearts on what is beyond their sight. Such fidelity could never be born in our hearts, nor could anyone be justified by faith, if our salvation lay only in what was visible. This is why Jesus said to his doubting apostle Thomas, who refused to believe unless he could see and touch the marks of his wounds in his very flesh, "Have you believed because you have seen me? Blessed are those who have not seen and yet have to believe" (Jn 20:29).

Because the Lord wanted all of us to be capable of this

kind of blessedness, he brought his visible presence among men to an end, until the period that God has fixed for the Christian people to increase and multiply is over. Then he will come again. In that same body in which he once submitted to the world's judgment, the world will see the Son of God coming as its Judge.

Meanwhile, our Redeemer has not left us orphans. His presence is always with us in the sacraments; in them we receive his living body and blood and his power is continually available to us. We no longer see him with our eyes, but our hearts have been enlightened by his grace. Our faith is purer and stronger because it is based on acceptance of the Spirit's teaching rather than on the message of our senses.

The faith of the infant Church was increased by the Lord's ascension and strengthened by the gift of the Spirit. It was to remain unshaken by fetters and imprisonment, exile and hunger, fire and ravening beasts, and the most refined tortures ever devised by brutal persecutors. Throughout the world women no less than men, girls as well as boys, have given their life's blood in the struggle for this faith. It is a faith that has cast out devils, healed the sick and raised the dead.

The miracles the Lord had worked among his disciples during his earthly life and all the teaching he had given them were not enough to save them from panicking at his crucifixion or from doubting his resurrection. Yet they made such progress as a consequence of his ascension that they now found joy in what had terrified them before. They found themselves able to fix their minds on their Lord and Master as he sat at the right hand of the Father, since they now realized that he had never left his Father when he came down to earth, nor had he abandoned them when he returned to heaven.

The fact is that the Son of Man was revealed as Son of God in a more perfect and transcendent way once he had entered into his Father's glory. His human companionship had been taken from them, but he was present to them now as God. Their faith had matured; now they could reach out in spirit to see him as the Father's equal. They no longer needed contact with his tangible body, in which as man he is less than the Father. By faith they could rise to heights where, as God's only Son, he is grasped not by physical handling but by spiritual discernment. This explains why Jesus said to his Church in the person of Mary Magdalene as she ran forward to cling to him in the garden: "Do not hold onto me, because I have not yet ascended to the Father" (Jn 20:17). In other words, I do not want you to come to me in this bodily way, to recognize me by what your senses tell you. I want you to wait for something higher. What I am preparing for you surpasses all such knowledge. When I have ascended to my Father and your Father, to my God and your God, then you will have an experience of me more real and perfect by far; you will grasp what you cannot touch at present and believe what you cannot see now.

THE COMING OF THE SPIRIT

"If I do not go away," Jesus told his apostles, "the Advocate will not come to you; but if I go, I will send him to you" (Jn 16:7). "While staying with them, he ordered them not to leave Jerusalem, but to wait there for the promise of the Father. 'This,' he said, 'is what you have heard from me, for

John baptized with water, but you will be baptized with the Holy Spirit not many days from now" (Acts 1:4-5).

These were the Lord's parting words to his disciples, the promise that united them as they made their way back to the city to wait in joyful, expectant faith for the coming of the Holy Spirit. Not that the Spirit would only begin to work among men after Jesus had returned to the Father; he had been at work in the world since the dawn of creation. God's people were not to experience a hitherto unknown indwelling of the Holy Spirit, but those who already belonged to him would know a more abundant outpouring, an increase rather than a first reception of his gifts.

Pentecost is the culmination of the work of our salvation, that mighty plan of God's mercy which originated long ago when the Lord first began to form a people for himself. How many mysterious signs can be discovered in this feast which link the old dispensation with the new, teaching us that the Law of Moses was the herald of the grace of Christ, in which it was to find its fulfillment! Fifty days after the sacrifice of the lamb marking the deliverance of the Hebrews from the Egyptians, the law was given to the people of Israel on Sinai; then fifty days from the resurrection of Christ, after his immolation as the true Lamb of God, the Holy Spirit came down upon the new Israel, the people who put their faith in Jesus. The same Holy Spirit was the author of both Old and New Testaments; the foundations of the gospel were laid with the establishment of the old covenant. What a wealth of meaning can be found, therefore, in the opening words of the second chapter of Acts, "When the day of Pentecost had come"!

Where the Spirit of the Lord is, there is freedom

> When the day of Pentecost had come, they were all together in one place. And suddenly from heaven there came a sound like the rush of a violent wind, and it filled the entire house where they were sitting. Divided tongues, as of fire, appeared among them, and a tongue rested on each of them. All of them were filled with the Holy Spirit and began to speak in other languages, as the Spirit gave them ability. (Acts 2:1-4)

No sooner had the Spirit come upon them than they began to speak in tongues. They needed no time to study the languages they were given, nor practice to gain facility. Nor did their hearers need an interpreter. God was the master of speakers and hearers alike; it was his Spirit that inspired the apostles to give testimony and enabled the crowds to understand them. That day the wonderful works of God were proclaimed in every language of the world. The Spirit of Truth breathes where he will, and since the day of Pentecost each country's native tongue has become common property in the mouth of Christ's Church, as the gospel is preached throughout the world. The Spirit of God has swept over the chaos once more to renew the face of the earth, watering every barren place with a rain of charismatic gifts and blessings. The tongues of nations declare God's mighty deeds and proclaim his word in the power of the Spirit, while the Lord works with them and confirms their message by accompanying signs (cf. Mk 16:20).

The perennial message of the gospel is that the Lord has saved his people. He has conquered sin and death, and given us new life as God's adopted children. And because we are his children, God has sent the Spirit of his Son into our hearts, crying, "Abba, Father!" (Gal 4:6). Now where the Spirit of the Lord is, there is freedom (2 Cor 3:17). We are no longer slaves, but free people. It belongs to the dignity of free people to play some part in their own salvation; our task is to elude the enemy's clutches by constantly turning in repentance to our Redeemer and proclaiming that Jesus is Lord of our whole lives.

SOURCES

Latin text in Migne, PL 54